The Classics in Paraphrase

The Classics in Paraphrase

Ezra Pound and Modern Translators
of Latin Poetry

Daniel M. Hooley

Selinsgrove: Susquehanna University Press
London and Toronto: Associated University Presses

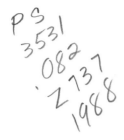

Associated University Presses
440 Forsgate Drive
Cranbury, NJ 08512

Associated University Presses
25 Sicilian Avenue
London WC1A 2QH, England

Associated University Presses
2133 Royal Windsor Drive
Unit 1
Mississauga, Ontario
Canada L5J 1K5

The paper used in this publication meets the requirements of the American
National Standard for Permanence of Paper for Printed Library Materials
Z39.48-1984.

Library of Congress Cataloging-in-Publication Data

Hooley, Daniel M.
  The classics in paraphrase.

  Bibliography: p.
  Includes index.
  1. Pound, Ezra, 1875–1972—Influence. 2. Pound, Ezra,
1875–1972. Homage to Sextus Propertius. 3. Latin poetry-
—Translations into English—History and criticism.
4. English poetry—Translations from Latin—History and
criticism. 5. Latin language—Translating into English.
6. Latin poetry—Paraphrases, tales, etc.—History and
criticism. 7. Poetry—Translating. I. Title.
PS3531.082Z648 1988   811'.52   86-43216
ISBN 0-941664-82-1 (alk. paper)

PRINTED IN THE UNITED STATES OF AMERICA

Contents

Preface

M Y notion as I began writing this little study was simply to examine translation as a means toward further understanding the role of classical models and influences in the development of modern poetry. Of course, with respect to the original poems of our major moderns, Pound, Eliot, Yeats, and the rest, uses of classical material had long been examined, *satis superque*. But I had come to feel that, with regard to the *general* perception of the classics in the long-ago days of nascent modernism, the very achievement of our preeminent poets, their singular creative accomplishment, tended to leave spectacular but ultimately false trails for critics to follow. Or trails leading to only partial truth. Translation, on the other hand, requires compromise, a muting of even a great and indomitable creative voice, in the service of some hoped-for synthesis, a joined and balanced articulation. The translator attends to his original, thinks about his relation to a classical poem and its meaning and pertinence in a changed world. That attention and thought, when it is exercised by the finest of our poets, offers intrinsic rewards to our scrutiny while deepening our understandings of the development of technique and idea in modern verse.

It might have been a happy chore, then, just to rummage through the myriad classical translations of our century's poets, and to try to make some sense of their ambitions and attainments. But Pound seems to have been right about great ages of literature coinciding with great ages of translation, and I was faced with a fearsome array of important works. In hasty retreat, I opted for something more modest: to begin on familiar ground by reexamining Pound's *Homage to Sextus Propertius* and to consider the "influence" (very broadly conceived) of that poem and its author among later translations of divers poets—though necessarily limited to a very few translations by a very few poets. This has not proved to be an occasion for setting out a systematic tabulation of translation techniques initiated by Pound and carried on by successors. That kind of study, however useful, might paint a distorting picture—giving Pound credit for a number of technical innovations not his at all (most of Pound's techniques are inherited) and casting others in the giant's shadow (for a generally well-done study of this nature, however, I can recommend Ronnie Apter's *Digging for the Treasure: Translation after Pound* [New York: Peter Lang, 1984]). The poets I discuss here are all well able to think for themselves and are not inclined to facile mimetic reaction; a few, in fact, think poorly of Pound. So we are faced with a situation considerably less neat but ultimately more interesting: that of a compulsive and ingenious translator doing something provocative with an ancient poem, which in turn has made others think about what they can do and how to go about it. And that, taken in sum, sheds a broad and general light not only on the relations of classical and modern literatures, but on the creative process as well; for these translators have made poems.

I have written the essays that follow from a literate layman's point of view, roughly that of Woolf's "common reader" (slightly the better if he or she has run across a little Latin in the course of life). Which means that specialists in classics or modern literature will find much of what I say elementary—particularly in my introduction. But since there are few specialists in both, the discussion may serve some purpose in establishing a common ground, a frame of mind, that can enable thinking about both literatures and their worlds together. To say that such mediating terms are more important to us, as readers and humans, than any circumscribed expertise may to some betray a nostalgic turn of mind. That is as may be, but I persist in contending that such terms do allow us, when we let them, a view of ourselves *through* time and thus present a fuller understanding of where we have come and how we have got here—some more complete sense of our humane culture. That sense, turned back to the poetry itself, demonstrates both the profound distance between classical and contemporary sensibilities and, paradoxically, the crucial perception that classical reading can thrive on (may need) the attention of a fertile and active modern imagination. My introductory chapter, in its desultory fashion, seeks, then, to provide one sort of commonality for questioning and thinking about these matters, while the ensuing chapters fill out our view with more focused literary analysis.

One kind of specialized talk will not be found much in evidence here. While my subject is translation and how writers think through and about it, I have not attempted to undertake a serious discussion of translation theory—though I do now and again make reference to theoretical ideas that I think are useful and fitting in a particular poetic circumstance. My conviction is that that is as far as any practical literary critic can go in a study of this kind without resigning a useful and healthy skepticism. Which is, of course, not to suggest that there may not be in the discussion that follows some ideas that impinge upon theory. One difference being that they will have been distilled through texts rather than received from on high. My bibliography will point those interested in the other side of things in some of the right directions.

One final point: although I have written this book for general readers—those interested in more than just classical poetry—I have refrained from offering my own translations of Latin and Greek passages lest they interfere, in the reader's eye, with the primary tension between original poem and version under discussion. A few short quotations remain untranslated, though they should be accessible to anyone with even a little Latin or the curiosity to look them up in a good translation, something more than the uninspiring crib I would, of necessity, offer. I hope few will be dismayed by such a procedure.

My debts are far too many to number here. I should at least begin by thanking my teachers and friends in classics and English literature. Among those, Thomas Clayton, Philip Furia, Elizabeth Belfiore, John Miller, George Sheets, and Robert Sonkowsky, have offered constant and intelligent support. Clay Jenkinson has turned his keen mind to parts of this, found some wanting, and gently let me know. W. R. Johnson has offered helpful criticism and generous encouragement, and J. P. Sullivan's acute scrutiny has eliminated several mistakes from the manuscript. Peter Firchow, though tolerant of my idiosyncracies of style and odd taste in poetry, has been my best and fiercest critic and has set me right countless times; the good bits here are his. The bad, all mine in impious despite.

I am happy to acknowledge the kindness of the following authors and publishers who have allowed me to reprint copyrighted material: Oxford University Press (Porter, Bunting), Jonathan Cape (Zukofsky), Ohio University Press (Cunningham), New Directions and Faber and Faber (Pound), Palmer Bovie, James Michie, University of Michigan Press (Rexroth), University of Texas Press (J. P. Sullivan's text of Pound's *Homage*). I must thank, too, the editors of *MLN*, *Sagetrieb*, and *Classical and Modern Literature* for permission to publish here what appeared there in other form.

The Classics in Paraphrase

Introductory Essay: Some Excursuses

> Better mendacities
> Than the classics in paraphrase!

POUND'S clinching phrase, in focusing momentarily upon translation, both embodies and displaces irony. The differences between "paraphrase" seen as a pedagogical tool—to explain the complex in simple terms—and as mutilated, degraded imitation are only variations on a theme. Both imply substantial diminution of complexity or value with, respectively (though not without shadings of admixture), positive and negative consequences. There is irony, then, in Pound's placement of these paraphrased classics as the "ideal" against which our vulgar age militates. But such irony is countered by the gestalt of literary history and nuance (of which Pound, especially Pound, was aware) embodied in the word. Dryden, as most know, saw "paraphrase" as a happy compromise between "imitation" and slavish, word-for-word translation, "metaphrase." Thus paraphrase paraphrased: "translation with latitude, where the author is kept in view by the translator so as never to be lost, but his words are not so strictly followed as his sense, and that too is admitted to be amplified, but not altered."[1] The spirit of Dryden is "kept in view" and "amplified" (though "altered" as well) by Walter Benjamin in "Die Aufgabe des Uebersetzers," his introduction to the translation of Baudelaire's *Tableaux parisiens:* "The language of a translation can—in fact, must—let itself go, so that it gives voice to the *intentio* of the original, not as reproduction but as harmony, as a supplement to the language in which it expresses itself, as its own kind of *intentio.*" The result, he continues, is that "translation" of this order will constitute the vital regeneration of a literary past, "a transformation of something living . . . so far from being the sterile equation of two dead languages that of all literary forms it is the one charged with the special mission of watching over the maturing process of the original language and the birth pangs of its own."[2]

But such large accomplishment is not always within easy reach, and the idea of literary regeneration raised for a moment in Pound's brief line is canceled by an ironic sense of the times:

> The "age demanded" chiefly a mold in plaster,
> Made with no loss of time,
> A prose kinema, not, not assuredly, alabaster
> Or the "sculpture" of rhyme.

To reconstrue the classics now is to construe them as one writes modern poetry, according to the demands, the authority, of the age. That is a facile truism, but the problems it presents to the translator are less obvious. The requirements of an age and the nature of a classic text are too often at fundamental odds—"prose kinema . . . alabaster"—and their translational synthesis an enormous difficulty. Pound registers in "Mauberley" as striking a disjunction of sensibilities as possible: the very roots of the western intellectual tradition (if we may be allowed that oversimplification for a moment)—"Attic grace, the sculpture of rhyme"—are set over against an alien present. Small wonder that "Mauberley" resolves itself in that failed aesthete's eloquent whimper.

But the prospect lingers in shadowy outline and has haunted the literary consciousness of our century. The scope of the concern can be nearly grasped if we, for a moment, extend our purview from translation to the whole range of modern literature that embodies elements from the classics. Immediately, even automatically, we are faced with the preeminent writers of modernism: Eliot, Joyce, Yeats, Pound, and Auden. Little need be said, anymore, about the role of Vergil and the Greek tragedians in *The Waste Land;* the structural and thematic importance of Homer in *Ulysses;* Pound's profound debt to Homer, Sappho, Catullus, Ovid, or even the contemned Pindar in the *Cantos;* the dependence upon classical mythology and lore in Auden and Yeats—all these have been explicated nigh to death. But what they represent is still vastly important to us, illustrating more than a simple or nostalgic reluctance to leave Horace's (and others') "momentum aere perennius" behind, as new science, new poetics, new visions propel us hastily onward. Instead, there is in these poets a sense of urgent need to provide fresh blood for the ghosts, to find and at least hear out again voices of the past, precisely because they are, in ways not yet fully explored, the voices of the present, still *mutatis mutandis,* somehow ours. After exploring a series of ephemeral personae, Pound can be said to have found "his" voice in his Englished Propertius; Joyce uses Homer compulsively in constructing his most idiomatic work; Eliot's verse, usually juxtaposing classical touchstones with diminished modern realities, infuses the ancient voices with a new kind of currency as the stable, ineradicable memory of intellectual and moral conscience. Nor need we focus on these exceptional figures. A similar preoccupation is manifest in the various searching "classicisms" of the main column of poets—the celebrated to the obscure—from the 1890s on: Lionel Johnson, Earnest Dowson, A. E. Housman, Thomas Hardy, Robert Trevelyan, Edgell Rickward, Richard Aldington, Hilda Doolittle, Robert Graves, Trumbull Stickney, Louis MacNeice, C. Day Lewis, Kenneth Rexroth, Basil Bunting, and C. H. Sisson among so many others.

It would be unfair to say that all of these writers (and more) were looking for the same things in their classical rummagings and equally unfair to generalize beyond the tentative comments already made about any particular author. Many deserve, and many have devoted to them, books on the subject. But the field of literary translations does constitute a more restricted and manageable aspect of this same general phenomenon: poets finding voices in their classical progenitors. Even with the rubric thus limited, fascinating material is superabundant: H. D.'s Sapphic fantasies, Richard Aldington's versions of Greek lyrics, Hardy's Sappho and Catullus, Housman's Horace, Allan Tate's *Pervigilium Veneris*, Kenneth Rexroth's selections from the Greek Anthology, MacNeice's Aeschylus, J. V. Cunningham's Martial and Catullus, W. S. Merwin's Persius, C. H. Sisson's Catullus, Ezra Pound's Propertius, Robert Lowell's Latin elegists, and more.

These poets in their use of translation suggest an issue of at least two complementary facets. The first, intimated above, pertains to translation as a means for more clearly and exactly understanding the role of the classical in modern literature and the relevance of past to present. Questions of generic and stylistic relationships, of philosophical contiguities, of the degree to which a revolutionary aesthetic is retro- as well as prospective, of the more broadly ideological and cultural implications of the modern turn to classical sources—these problems are in some ways most precisely and satisfactorily answered by a look at the relatively confined and controlled situation translation presents. The second and obverse facet of the phenomenon represented by these poets is the intriguing conception of translation as an element, a component, of a certain kind and order of *poiesis*. This follows notions often expressed in contemporary theory that, in one case, describes translation not as a representation of an original text, but as an "influenced articulation through further utterance."[3] That is, as a creative and assertive rather than derivative activity. This view of translation obviously has implications of a broad and central importance vis-à-vis the entire poetic process and requires some attention.

Examples abound and across great sweeps of time tell essentially the same story. Twenty centuries ago Catullus was translating Sappho and Callimachus and in so doing was allowing us a glimpse into the operations of his own creative intellect and, consequently, into the heart of his poetry as a whole. Sixteen centuries later Marlowe was composing his magnificent version of Lucan, which, placed in relation to his sportive Ovid, offers real insight into the workings of that mysterious Renaissance mind. Translation thus seen as a manifestation of the creative impulse will often imply radical revision of a source text. This would have come as no surprise to Horace or to Catullus who suggest as much explicitly and through metaphorical indirection in their verse. But it is particularly compelling to modernist poetics, which has generated so profoundly extreme a reformulation of the classics. H. D.'s dreamy revisions of Sappho and her imagist's Greek tragedy, Louis Zukofsky's scarcely intelligible homophonic experiments with Catullus,

Browning's premodernist but famously eccentric Aeschylus represent just the edge of a movement that has manhandled the classics in an effort to wrest from them something to suffice now. So it is that Ezra Pound's powerful reading of the elegies of Sextus Propertius, while illuminating the most abiding, even "modern," qualities of the Latin poet's temperament and art, uses the occasion of translation for setting out the very elements of an aesthetic that was to account for "Hugh Selwyn Mauberley" and the early *Cantos*—his most extraordinary and influential works. Indeed it is Pound's classical translations or rather Pound *translating* that provides for our century one of its most seminal conceptual models, one of its most characteristic poetic personae. Its importance in providing an intellectual focus for the modern era is difficult to overstate and provides some unexpected confirmation of Kenner's otherwise hyperbolic phrase, "the Pound era."[4]

*   *   *

> Nor can I do better, in conclusion, than impress upon you the study of Greek literature, which not only elevates above the vulgar herd, but leads not infrequently to positions of considerable emolument.
>
> —Dean Gaisford, last century.

> God knows why it should be so, but as a matter of observation it seems to me quite certain that the whole legend of the "English Gentleman" has been built upon Latin and Greek. A. meets B. on the steps of his club and says, "Well, old man, *eheu fugaces,* what?" and B. says, *"Dulce et decorum est pro patria mori,"* and the crossing-sweeper falls on his knees in adoration of the two men who can talk as learnedly as that.
>
> —Ronald Knox[5]

Any discussion of creative translation of classical literature in the first half of the twentieth century will reflect some awareness of the "unique" situation in which our century finds itself in its severance from a once-central literary and cultural tradition. There can be little more to add to a subject that has become a commonplace of criticism beyond, perhaps, a little perspective on how it all bears on the reception (and perception) of classical letters in our day. It is of course readily apparent that training in the classics has lost its privileged position in English and American education. The causes are numerous and obvious: the natural pressure of ever-diversifying fields of knowledge, the emergence and dominance of the sciences and practical disciplines in modern life, the "leveling" influences of universal education that work against traditional programs oriented toward an economic elite, the rather sudden rise in the study of national literatures and languages that began to define and transmit, in F. R. Leavis's phrase, the "central humanity." And so on. In England the criticisms of classical dominance of the Victorian curriculum voiced by Sydney Smith, Whewell, Spencer, T. H. Huxley, and even Henry Sidgwick played only a small part in the general momentum. As early as 1868, the report of the *Inquiry into Grammar Schools* noted that Greek had almost disappeared from schools in the north of England and decided that this was not such a bad thing. Greek really suited only those going on to university. Latin might stay—until a suitable replacement could be found. Up to the turn of the century—in some cases a little later—a typical public school syllabus through the sixth form might include, along with a variety of introductory primers and prose composition texts in both languages, Caesar, Xenophon, Aristophanes, Vergil, Thucydides, Plato, Aeschylus, Ovid, Cicero, Homer, Euripides, and Lucretius. A comparable American school might require Caesar, Cicero, Vergil, Xenophon, Homer, Plato, Herodotus, and Thucydides.[6] Such curricula no longer exist on any scale below college or university level and often not even there, while the numbers of students involved with them on any level is drastically reduced. In determining this course of affairs, the period 1880–1920 was decisive, as it was in so many other respects, with the result that systematic transmission of inherited "tradition," the salient bits of humane learning, were made available to (or forced upon) progressively fewer and fewer.

In spite of such obvious and momentous trends, classical scholarship during the same period had developed impressively, and again, the mid-Victorian period to the turn of the century registered, perhaps, the most startling advances. The archaeological renaissance, popularly catalyzed by the discoveries of Schliemann,[7] resulted in the recovery of important papyri from desert sands. "New" classical literature came under scrutiny, and some, like the programmatic passages of Callimachus, were strikingly important for literary studies. Along similar lines, new techniques of textual analysis and restoration substantially improved and extended our knowledge of the corpus of such major lyricists as Sappho and Pindar. In the study of classical history, Theodor Mommson mounted a revolution of sorts ultimately resulting in radical changes in historical methodology and, eventually, in a far more precise picture of the ancient artist's context. And, too, in the latter half of the nineteenth century literary research of a certain analytical sort reached unprecedented levels of sophistication and excellence—particularly in Germany. Those labors, and the fruits of same, reflected a depth of enthusiasm, a comprehension of the intricacies of literary relationship (viz. the emphasis on *Quellenforschung*), of linguistic and lexical ranges, of genre description and definition that still provides the informational and methodological core of modern classical studies. The same energy for research and documentation in this period resulted in a remarkable improvement of classical resource materials and text quality and availability.[8]

Two trajectories, then: advanced scholarship over against general currency—one ascending, one falling, meeting at the cusp of the centuries. The forces of science and new knowledge, just as they have made our world smaller and tamer, have, for some, constricted the gap of years, and certain details of the classical past of two millennia gone seem startlingly near to us. But for most of us the drift of time and change really is irrevocable, the rhythms of thinking and living, in past and present, irreconcilably at odds:[9] "The past is a foreign country; they do things differently there."[10] We can be certain that the consequences of such a dramatic turning away are deeply significant. Not ever has the prospect of living in an essentially pastless society, in which the guiding visions of the age emanate almost exclusively from the promises of a technologically defined, proleptically oriented *telos,* seemed to imminent. All aspects of culture are touched by such developments, of course, but in literature the effects are uncommonly dramatic. Conventionally bound to a tradition that has lost its ability effectively to signify, it finds itself under a remarkable strain. Even a cursory look at the list of major modernist figures cited near the beginning of this essay will remind us that our sense of literary and cultural history is neither simply amnesiac nor gracefully allusive in the old style in its use of the literary past. Rather there is an urgency in its tone, a need to reestablish continuities or to break off hard, in the vividness of experiment. So Joyce uses Ulysses to gloss Bloom, and Eliot the Theseus and Ariadne myth and the murder of Agamemnon to juxtapose and valorize modern barroom vulgarity.

Yet these are general tendencies in a complex and turbulent situation. Not all artists are going to respond in precisely this way. What we can be certain of is that these were for the early twentieth century, and are, major issues of the day; that although we have been addressing the relatively circumspect domain of "the classics," there is little doubt that modernism's response to this literature, a powerfully interfusing conjunction of forces, has a real importance. To this we will return, but one prominent aspect of our modern condition demands more immediate attention: the role of translation. If one is able to gain insight into an age by noting what it does with and thinks about its literary past, a history of its translations should be doubly revelatory. For in the latter case, the interaction of old and new is more immediate and the issues of expression, tone, and attitude more naked. Here several factors will be informative. For the sheer number and stylistic variety of its classical translations, the first half of our century ranks with the Renaissance and the age of Pope. That fact not only reflects the recurrence of certain social and literary conditions that provoke revisionary or retrospective moments in history but also suggests a parallel between translation activity and the kind of searching intellectual energy that characterizes the brightest efflorescences of English literary achievement. Yet, to say so is not to maintain that these flurries of translation interest are merely part of an inevitable rhythm of historical pattern or that the specific factors precipitating such periods are essentially similar. They are not. The Renaissance translated (when it wasn't translating the Bible) out of an authentic and enthusiastic desire to reinfuse life with classical values, as they saw them, and to invigorate English letters with the sophisticated literary forms, the highly developed styles, and the vast learning of "newly emergent" classical texts. Energy, optimism, and enthusiasm, combined almost contradictorily with a love of literalism born of the high value placed on these texts, characterized their efforts. The eighteenth century was more retrospective and self-conscious: a mature literary culture beginning to question, to revise, to manipulate classical material often in ironic ways. Translation theory came to the fore: a secondary activity that testified to the "belated" and reflective intellectual tenor of the period.

The twentieth century translates out of still other motives. Need is a primary factor, as it always has been. But whereas the past could rely on the "originals" to provide an unbroken, if limited and privileged, continuity of significant literary artifacts, our century even among its educated classes cannot.[11] Translation comes near to being the final appeal—in obvious ways a substitute for the classical text: a substitute providing both the "information" and something analogous to the "artistic experience" of the poem. The day of the utilitarian crib is largely gone.[12] This double-faceted need provides for the most ambitious and serious of our modern translations: there can be no reason, however one feels about freedoms taken or final "success," to dismiss such work lightly. Many of our translators are fine poets, and their translations, if now and again controversial, often employ sophisticated scholarship and a perceptive eye in making the things they do. Not a few in one way or another speak to us in clear, hard language that still signifies with an epic grandeur or lyric intensity.

But reasons beyond excellence compel interest in the translator-poets of our century. For these, along with many of the major poets of premodernism and modernism itself, were experimenters, looking at times almost desperately for some different place or relevancy for the classics. Desperate may not be too strong a word, for instance, for Samuel Butler's "discovery" of comedy and satire in, and feminine authorship of, Homer's epics (reflected in his translations of 1898 and 1900 as well as in the famous published scholarship). This search for new insight and application describes a second major motive of the time. For the prospect of two languages and literatures that had for more than two millennia provided the central visions and intellectual patterns of a civilization passing into obsolescence had created, these artists realized, two alternative possibilities, two potential literary "conditions." The first we have discussed: the progressive segregation of classical literatures from ordinary and even fairly rarified intellectual life. But another response, premised on the assumption that some such segregation has already taken place, has presented itself to a few: classical material, if seen and treated in certain ways, could represent new knowledge and the stuff of new poetry. The curious fact, as D. S. Carne-Ross has written, is that the breakdown in continuity described above has ironically conferred upon classical literature an almost unprecedented novelty.[13] This is true not only in the obvious sense of any individual coming into contact with any piece of literature for the first time but also in the deeper sense of a fresh, even alien, frame of reference and mind, an entire gestalt of literary context, that is suddenly "there" for us and calls for inquiry and understanding.[14] This startling inversion of temporal continuity, where past and future are syn- thesized conceptually, was initially explored by certain modernist poet- translators in the first three decades of our century—Pound, H. D., Richard Aldington, and others—and has been continued to the present by their successors: Tate, Day Lewis, MacNeice, Merwin, Cunningham, Rexroth, et al. It has even filtered down into critical writing where we find semiotics, deconstruction, hermeneutics, and "new" rhetorics based terminologically and often conceptually upon classical learning.[15] Even educational fashion is affected, and we have seen proposals (though followed by little action) to reintroduce Greek and Latin studies on a broad scale—not necessarily out of nostalgic yearnings for the old high road, but because they provide access to frames of reference, manners of thinking, that *may* liberate the modern reader from the now hidebound intellectual habits of a post-classical age.[16]

The validity of such programs is open to question, of course, but it is impossible to gainsay the ironic fact that our movement away from any kind of general classical literacy since the turn of the century has given rise to novel ways of thinking about old poems. And this kind of "innocence," having become characteristic, accounts for rather different ways of engaging past and future, of modifying, in Auden's phrase, the words of dead men "in the guts of the living." With the "laws" of chronology and influence appar- ently disrupted (as one could now look prospectively into the past), the literary heritage became less a burden and a curse than a terra incognita, an intellectual geography rendered strange and new, a possibility. Exploring that possibility became one of the hallmarks of modernism. In translation, this phenomenon can be yet more vividly seen and especially in the transla- tions of Pound and those affected by him. Their achievement, which will be discussed in some detail below, is not easy to measure or describe: the problem they approach and the ways they do it simply haven't occurred in exactly these terms before. But it needs to be described: no full understand- ing of the period's literature is possible without it. It is broadly this phenom- enon—translator-poets demonstrating in the manner of their engagement with old poems some terribly acute awareness of their position in time and culture and art, of their being simultaneously at an end of things and a beginning—that one refers to in describing Pound and his circle as seminal moderns, however inconsistent their respective programs and attainments.

And the issues they first adumbrate will occupy the center of our attention, even as they develop and diversify in successors.

⁂ ⁂ ⁂

But such issues must be seen, here, through the overlay of translation itself, and that, unto itself, is a slippery and protean thing—a phenomenon whose dimensions shift under the pressure of critical attention. The informative histories of translation theory written by Louis Kelly, George Steiner, and others have given us a clear sense of the difference perspective makes. A scholar with ties to the German hermeneutic tradition, like Benjamin, may see translation as a creative, even mystical act. A linguist or semiotician may see the same activity as the rearrangement of differential bits of language and compensatory readjustments within respective semiotic systems. A philosopher of language might seek to speculate about the peculiar character language takes on during translation or about the absolute "possibility" of the enterprise.[17] And on. All, through their varieties of perspective and approach, contribute something to our understanding of the terribly complicated issues involved. My intention, however, is not to analyze translation per se extensively and exhaustively, and thus to come up with another privileged theoretical picture, but to look at what it does in an essentially literary situation. This, in an era of theory, may seem to some an evasion. But an often overlooked truth is that the practice of translation is born of and bound up with a more complete, if more intuitive, view of the issues than any secondary theory. It is further true, whether we like it or not, that translators do what they will, not attending much to what critics and specialists of one kind or another say about them, and usually lead the way into new conceptual ground.

Pound is a classic example in this as in so much. His remarks on translation are thick enough on the ground to qualify him as a kind of theorist. But he lacks system. His lengthy comments in his introduction to the Cavalcanti translations discuss things quite other than those he speaks of in "Notes on Elizabethan Classicists" and "Translators of Greek." There is enough coherence for a historian of translation like Kelly to ascribe to him a "position"—and one that is surely accurate enough.[18] Still in all, he is in this scheme of things minor, and rightly enough no one pays much attention. But Pound is a better poet than theorist and consequently a better thinker within the limits and through the texture of his verse. Imbedded within that texture is a formidable variety—Cavalcanti, Li Po, the "Seafarer," Andreas Divus's Homer, Ovid, Propertius, Horace, and much more—none of these doing quite the same things or engineered toward the same ends. But in some cases, the Propertius conspicuously, Pound seems to have arrived at a new formulation of the terms of literary translation, one that subsequent thinkers about either the poetry or the science of the translator's practice must take into consideration. Indeed, some of the difficulties encountered in discussions of Pound's Propertius derive from a failure to recognize this.[19] A story to be taken up later.

One general theme that proceeds directly from Pound's work with Propertius and is followed up by a good many others may be mentioned here. That is the notion of translation as a means of literary inquiry. It is of course a commonplace that translation involves interpretation—virtually all abstract models of the art involve a component that accounts for it. So too are the points of debate in translation and critical exegesis parallel: re-presentations of an author's "intention"' the distinction (Hirsch's) between intended "meaning" and interpreted "significance"; the text's plurality in and through time; its indeterminacy or secrecy; the role of the reader in "coproducing" a text—all these either play a direct role in translation theory or have clear analogues there. A good many of the major literary theoreticians and critics of our day—Barthes, Derrida, Kristeva, Jakobson, Steiner, Cluysenaar, Davie, Scholes, Eagleton—are frequently invoked or take on active roles in debates and discussions of translation.[20] But it is one thing to say that translators must be interpreters to do their job well and quite another to consider translation, *ab extra*, a particularly valuable sort of hermeneutic technique. This is perhaps the more strikingly so in the rather prescribed context of rendering the Latin and Greek classics. Their distance in time and cultural situation is so great that simply understanding the words literally does us little good. Yet they are so crucially a part of our heritage, our half-forgotten selves, that they always, subtly, almost imperceptibly, impinge upon our conscious lives. This means that they are continuously *proposing* themselves, requiring acknowledgement and some role in our intellectual and emotional capacities—something not entirely true of the contemporary literatures we translate. Acknowledgement demands a degree of understanding, which is to say that we need to know not what they say, but what they mean. And "meaning" in this context is precisely the concurrence and engagement of different sensibilities, an almost literal touching of minds past and present. Classical translation, then, is a fusion of interrogative and declarative modes; but interrogation predominates and a translation "declares" only as an hypothesis within a larger question: will this suffice as a token of our comprehension?

The actual configuration of each translation's interrogation will be different from any other; that is one reason it is so hard to talk sensibly about translation in general. But all will attempt to sort through the problem of a classical text's immanence. That last word suggests at least a mildly conservative point of view in some of the ongoing debates about the nature of literature. But the point is that more is involved than poems conceived in relation to semiotic fields, as enduring or deconstructing arrangements of abstract signs. Those poems are clearly, too, manifestations of temperament, not only the linguistic traces of men and women long dead but formal expressions of their thought and feeling. The life of Propertius is there in his poems—for us it is only there; Martial's emotional incapacities live still in his gynephobic epigrams, as his healthier wit lives in the others; Ovid's literary strength is omnipresent, his weakness of resolve and pathos come unmitigated to us in the *Epistulae ex Ponto;* there is everywhere the doubt of Vergil the man in the shattering sensitivity that pervades his long epic. A translation of a classical text must therefore "bear in mind" more than a text's signifying processes; rather it asks through and around their semiosis about the minds and now estranged worlds that made them, for they are part of what the words mean.

But that meaning, compound as it is, is further complicated by our brave new world which does strange new things to it. Aeneas may to us seem to simper, although no Roman could so conceive him.[21] Thus we must think through our condition, understand what has happened to ourselves as well as the poem. The translational formula, then, is in constant flux. When it derives an answer from the poem that is its inquiry, that response is like one of Augustine's syllables, gone nearly in the moment of utterance or passed into the storage of literary-cultural memory, there to take on a different character. Which means that translation cannot afford definitive exegesis; it is not the interpretation of either the philological scholar or the historically-minded critic. It is rather the record of a moment's insight, surrounded by perceptions of other instants, before and after, and so is part of a process that marks out the dimensions of a text's mutability in time.[22]

But it is true that in years past translation has investigated its texts and recognized its differences in time with a kind of dreary sameness of method. The terminology critics have developed to describe its techniques—"formal correspondence" and "dynamic equivalence," "découpage," "incorporation," "restitution," "modulated transposition," "refraction," and the rest don't suggest so much a variety of methods as a creative variety in ways of talking about them. Kelly, near the close of his history of translation theory, has it that "the repertoire of translation techniques has not evolved: there is little to choose between Cicero and Pound in range of dynamic technique." He further concludes that "sophisticated modern analyses have not affected the practice of translation at all deeply" (1978, 226).

But there may be a sense in which Kelly's view accounts for only part of the present situation, a sense in which there is in fact *something* to choose between Cicero and Pound. Which is to recognize that the two don't at all ask the same kinds of questions of their texts and that the freedom of their "dynamic" techniques (Eugene Nida's term, which he opposes to "formal," more nearly literal correspondences[23]) gets turned to quite different ends. This matters most vis-à-vis classical texts. So that Pound in translating Propertius is not merely employing dynamic means to construct an "equivalency" of a sort but is instead using the muscle of English to find something in the Latin hitherto ignored. He demonstrably succeeds in this. The ligaments of Propertius's irony are pulled and tested to their limits; could they bear the burden of Pound's anti-imperial sentiments? They could, and the poems, even in the Latin, are stronger for it. The crucial notion is of a modern language probing the old, pushing it to its extremes, discovering its expressive resiliency. And so, learning more from it.

E. S. Shaffer, citing Schliermacher, outlines the beginnings of a case for translation (and translation studies) as a methodological alternative to the defunct New Criticism, even while it preserves some of the dominant techniques of close reading and *explication de texte:*

> [T]hrough translation is revealed the multiplicity of the interpretations of the poetological construction of the author. . . . Comparative literary studies suggest a solution to the dilemmas posed by the banishing of the national modes of close reading. In the most recent books on comparative literary theory, while 'close analysis' is omitted as before, 'Translation' has become an essential heading, under which detailed analyses are now being conducted. . . . For the development of a theory of translation as *aisthesis* or poetological construction, literary hermeneutics and semiotics offer fresh scope, and both indicate a broader framework within communication theory.[24]

Shaffer's faith in the advancements of "a" theory of translation "as *aisthesis* or poetological construction" may strike some as optimistic, but the perception underlying it—that the art has begun to be seen as a potent critical tool—is sound. One may doubt its ability ever to become systematically methodological, as, say, an established hermeneutic technique, without gainsaying its efficacy in penetrating to secret and surprising meaning. Indeed, the asystematic multiplicity of approach, as poets investigate poems in their own ways, towards their own ends, is essential to the diversity of impression and effect that is the translator's exegetical strength. So it is that in the (quite unsystematic) essays that follow, I have not tried to make the poets covered seem as if they were doing or working toward the same things. They all "translate" under the broadest interpretation of the term; that is, create a poem "for which another poem is its *raison d'être.*"[25] But beyond translating, each poet works to his own purpose in his own way, makes the thing he loves. I have tried to follow their leads as they have turned now here, now there, as poets will, and I've not tried to construe them as part of the progress of "communication theory." Yet in sum they are different from their predecessors; they have turned translation into one kind of cognitive tool, heuristic device, so that the reproduction of sense matters less than insight achieved. Translation has become not a mode of conservation but a means to register positive gain and enlightenment.

In Pound and a good many subsequent translators may be seen, then, neither a resipiscence to the same old translational conceptions nor the fulfillment of a progressive evolution, but a shift in conceptual frequency. In each case there may be observed, in the making of a poem (and equally "making something of" another and ancient poem) a record of private construal, hypersensitive and intensely inquisitive, laid open to us, provoking the old languages to touch us again with sudden luminescence. So, in Logue's Homer:

> Though it is noon, the helmet screams against the light;
> Scratches the eye: so violent it can be seen
> Across three thousand years.

But something further separates translation's construals from those of ordinary (or extraordinary) criticism. It *confronts* its text differently. The language of criticism (whatever the brand of the moment) is usually confined to analytical prose—not the language of art. Its discourse is often directed toward specialists of some sort or other rather than "readers in general" (it is far from certain that readers of critical theory and analysis are enthusiastic readers of poems, and vice versa). Which is not (so much) to say that readers of one group or another are wrong, but that the "level" and communicative purpose of the respective discourses are strikingly different. That is in one sense a good thing. Criticism's attempts to bring across something of poetry into *its* language, however imperfectly, suggest an effort to broaden poetry's intelligibility and comprehension. But the limits are real. Criticism examines a poem in its own terms, terms in which the poem itself is essentially mute. The poem communicates "generally," but in the discourse it defines for itself, finally, in the most important ways, only its own.

Yet the resistance of the work of art to inspection may be lessened a bit via translation. Naturally enough, like the poem, translation is a poetically "expressive" mode of language. Its audience, too, is general. Rather than selectively investigate, deconstruct, a poem's composition, it seeks (broadly) to "repeat" in some manner analogous to that of the original. That that repeating must involve critical effort we have already noted, but the fact that its communicative goals and energies are largely the same as those of the original work accounts for a necessarily deeper intimacy between the two, a nearer access to the poem's privacy. Which is to say that even bad translation, when it seeks artistic re-presentation, is closer to some (only some) features of the poem's intent than is the most learned scholarship. The simple sharing of poetic voice demonstrably and often yields more than the scholar's magisterial knowledge of language, circumstance, and poetic device.

The situation, insofar as it may puzzle us still, is worth a moment's further thought. For in understanding the translator's unique "grasp" upon a poem, one must realize that the relation between text and translation is not merely that of a prior and more valuable work "imitated" by another that is secondary and less valuable. Thus it is not only a matter of "first this, then that"—the sequentiality of which has effectively determined the configurations of most translation theory to date (although naturally enough). Such a diachronic model fails to account for a crucial aspect of the translation process that is precisely synchronic: the translating poet must, in the composition of his version, hold both texts in mind, in a kind of synthetic, creative present. The translation of a poem is never merely a matter of substituting word for word but a manipulation of the elements of language within terribly complex expressive systems as these are held in a subtle and difficult kinetic balance. To alter a word in a translation is not only to change the proportions and character of the translation's composition but as well its relation, on the level of word and semiotic system, to the original. Which is to say that the translated poem is not considered, in this artificial present, as a historical artifact; its antiquity, its manifold contingencies to the life of its times—these exist only, as it were, behind the poem's primary force as illocutionary act. At *this* moment (others involving the usual scholarly and historical concerns will precede and follow it), the poem is conceived only as an articulatory presence.

Oddly enough, this feature of the translating process—although its effects are everywhere evident—remains substantially unexamined. It has been mentioned that the translator as opposed to the critic speaks and thinks in terms essentially those of their original poets. Even if the two manifest wildly various attitudes toward their verse, the manners of their language are those of disciplined poetic articulation. Further, the translator must balance his voice over against that of his precursor and in so doing gives both poems a degree of openness, a kinetic interconnectedness they have not had before nor will after. They are "new" together, joined in a composite intertextuality. In a very real sense, both, for this moment, are part of a compounded semiotic system in which both poem and translation (as it is being generated) partake mutually in a singular expressive act. At this stage of fluid interconnectedness, the texts "react" to one another. The translation in obvious ways to the poem; but the original as well, in the ways that texts *will* respond—differently to the different kinds of questions asked of it. And the point is that the translation must, in its slow and difficult incarnation, as a matter of pragmatic method, ask new questions at every turn. These questions draw out a series of responses that will account for the evolving character of the translation. It is a process that will take into its reckoning several "Aeneids," for example, and several translations. At this point, where the translation engages a variety of impressions of the text, there is no question of a fixed and certain, singularly signifying original nor any question of reproducing that original's "singular signification." One will find no clearer demonstration of the mutability inherent in literary work, in reading and writing.

But then will come a return to time, when the translated poem is drawn out of its artificial copresence with its original. Here again, there will be a commerce between the two texts, but conducted in other terms. Each poem is "placed" in its historical and social context, and the translator is concerned with arranging a correspondence between the two that makes sense of their diachronic relation. That relation will again be fluid, dynamic. Thus, although Latin and Greek are dead enough as languages these days and although their antiquity is a primary feature of their "character" as media for ideas and verse, the translator cannot afford to consider them inert or ossified. He is bound to ask what "meaning" in the poem is pliant enough to survive the years and what has changed since its composition (or last translation) to alter its very significance. This dialogue between poem and translation may be barren, may yield little of note or interest to the reader. That is as translations often are—just bad. But there are translations that make much of this process of intertextual composition, translators who make evident in the translation they create the conspiracy to greater collaborative significance that is in fact the "reason" of the translation's final form.

This active interrelation of texts, along both synchronic and diachronic axes, will be seen variously in divers translations. Pound will modulate these interactions by means of a literary persona that mediates the respective intentions of the two poets precisely on this level of linguistic synchronicity and which can be seen to exercise its control over the translation's composition—differently (and that is important) in its different sections. Zukofsky will strangely reconfigure the sense of his Catullus in order to point to deeper, more interesting ways in which the poem and translation share expressive intents. J. V. Cunningham, likewise, though far more conservatively in manner, will reflect in his translations of Martial a most vivid sense of dialogue, of meaning building upon meaning. And others in other ways, which will become evident only if one looks at the poems a little less conventionally. Only if one shakes off the persistent idea that translations merely "follow" in time and intention their originals. To do that, one must look hard at both poems to see how they impinge upon and diverge from each other, to discover the translation's genesis in the early, volatile interactions of "texts" and their moments of shared articulation.

One further thing. These modern translations not only unfold ancient ideas to modern understanding while making evident the compounded polyphony of poem and version, but do so in a way that transcends their textuality, that turns it, in fact, to an exploration into the dimensions of real experience, past and present. The translating poet locates pattern in the traces of echo and shadow that are left to us and through them effects a deepening of our awareness of the boundedness of life and art. Thus, the shades he raises to our ken from long ago, strange though they be, will have a familiar and lively look to them. The better to become acquainted.

1

Pound's Propertius Again

THERE is more than a little danger in too often reading a poem in the same light, in always approaching by the easy and familiar path. No exception is Pound's *Homage to Sextus Propertius*, which from the date of its publication to virtually the present moment has excited lively and amusing controversy centering primarily on its qualities and integrity *qua* translation. At times, the debate has reached such a pitch that intelligent and decorous analysis has given way to passionate and indecorous polemic. This is not all bad; poetry ought to affect people in the visceral ways Pound's translation has. But the issue, in the terms hitherto suggested, is probably irresolvable. In essence, Pound has written a poem that in obvious ways depends upon and translates selected portions of the Propertian corpus, even while it alters some of that Propertius beyond all recognition. What does one call this? To call it translation is to invite criticism on grounds of inaccuracy. Plenty of that. To think it no translation at all but rather an original poem, as Donald Davie has, is manifestly implausible: one simply can't wish the Latin poem away.[1] To take the middle road, as J. P. Sullivan has done, and call it creative translation along lines dictated by Johnson and Fitzgerald, invites criticism from both extremes, particularly in its logically necessary attempts to elevate what appear to be errors into patterns of calculated ironic distortion.[2]

These are the themes of the *Homage* criticism to date, and they and their variations are no doubt destined to a long half-life.[3] For the single indisputable fact is that the poem is stubbornly there before us, whatever one calls it, and its power to compel or irritate its readers remains undiminished. The prognosis of Robert Conquest, made twenty years ago, has not held: "One can predict that, like Mussolini's, this bullfrog reputation will soon have faded entirely. It should not be very long before the student of literary curiosities is alone interested in such residual questions as (in the Duke of Wellington's words) who will Pound longest."[4] But then the ferocity of his attack on Pound and the Propertius in particular ought to have betrayed to Conquest the limits of his own wishful thinking and suggested the centrality of Pound to the modern imagination in ways his alternative canon (E. Thomas, Blunden, Flecker, Cameron, Chesterton, Housman, de la Mare are his candidates) cannot approach. His own passionately negative response to the *Homage,* in short, ought to have warned him of the folly of wishing Tremenheere's version more read than Pound's.

And so the danger of falling into such difficulties looms large when one, again, begins to discuss this poem in the context of translation. But the situation still needs putting into some perspective. One could begin with translation theory, which has its place here, especially in light of its remarkable efflorescence during our century—Richards, Benjamin, Firth, Nida, Levý, Mounin, Toury, Catford, Steiner, Kelly, among many others have offered significant insights and join the company of a relatively few important figures from the preceding two millennia: Cicero, Quintilian, Augustine, Jerome, Erasmus, Luther, Cowley, Dryden, Pope, Campbell, Tytler, Goethe, Arnold.[5] But in spite of the proliferation of contemporary theory and its fearsome technical apparatus and vocabulary, Steiner is correct in pointing to the essential if perhaps too-simple truth of Ronald Knox's summary: "Knox reduces the entire topic to two questions: which should come first, the literary version or the literal; and is the translator free to express the sense of the original in any style and idiom he chooses?"[6] That is to say, these are the practical and functional questions the translator has always asked himself. Cicero did; so too Stephen MacKenna.

Such plain pragmatism fetches along another old warhorse not quite dead: a translation is "literal" or "free" or somewhere between. Sometimes, especially since Dryden and more lately Lowell, "imitation" or "version" is used to describe extreme freedom, a fantasia. Clearly, it is nearer this end of the descriptive scale that Pound's Propertius belongs. Neither the sophisticated precisions of linguistics nor the almost sacramental pronouncements of a Walter Benjamin will change that homespun fact.[7] So, for all the supersubtle analyses of the mechanisms and intents of Pound's lexical and syntactic exchange to be published in years to come as theory becomes more advanced and dominant, the *Homage* will never be intrinsically anything other than it is for the ordinary reader now—a remarkably (and remarkable) free translation.

Such a designation would not have bothered Pound. But the adverse criticism from the classicist Hale, from the *New Age* reviewer,[8] and from the other early fault finders[9] *did* bother Pound and finally drove him to renounce the term "translation" altogether: "No, I have not done a translation of Propertius" (*Letters,* 245). This is in spite of his clearly different frame of mind before and during the poem's composition, as the frequently cited letter in 1916 to Iris Barry shows: "And if you CAN'T find any decent translations of Catullus and Propertius, I suppose I shall have to rig up something." Pound's surprise, then, his being taken aback by public reaction so far and so drastically, is compelling: "I am unable to imagine a depth of stupidity so great as to lead Miss Monroe or the late Hale into believing that I supposed I had found an allusion to Wordsworth or a parody of Yeats in

Propertius. . . . Hale's criticism displayed not only ignorance of Latin but ignorance of English" (*Letters*, 310). The sudden resort to invective, the tone of dogmatic pronouncement that was to characterize so much of his later writing, the fierce indignation, suggest real and substantial shock, a mind cast back upon its most primitive defenses. It is commonly known that in these situations denial is instinctive (so Desdemona and the handkerchief). "My *Homage To Sextus Propertius* is not a translation of Propertius."

But why? Certainly Pound knew of at least most of the liberties he was taking with his original. Pedants could be expected to object and should be easy to dismiss. But virtually all of Pound's early reactions seem those of a man caught out, *in flagrante*. The defensiveness is a matter of record. The pretensions to full academic equipment: "The quarrel over 'Punic' was started before your reviewer came upon it, and the ancient vestiges of my pedantry beget phantom figures to fill them." The jaded sophistication: "I am tired, very tired, of Amphion and of lyres, whether of tortoise-shell or some less brittle compost." The resentment: "The philologists have so succeeded in stripping the classics of interest that I have already had more than one reader who has asked me, 'who was Propertius?'" (1919, 82–83). What is fascinating about this reaction is that it seems to want to justify the *Homage* along the lines of "conventional" translation. No exulting in the delightful fantasies he worked on Propertius, but shrill posturing and claims that his was somehow the "true" Propertius. Surely, his effort to defend, say,

> And you, O Polyphemus? Did harsh Galatea almost
> Turn to your dripping horses, because of a tune, under Aetna?
> We must look into the matter.

in terms chiefly dictated by his critics, as he seems to do throughout his long letter to the *New Age* and elsewhere, is at the very least extremely puzzling. Finally, of course, the rubric "translation" was abandoned, and Sullivan (1964, 10) is correct in noting that this was a perfectly understandable protective step. But Pound's initial reaction reveals much, for it points to his operating conception of what a translation ought to be—before adverse criticism drove him to renunciation. And with this as a guide, in spite of the apparently revolutionary character and power of the *Homage*, we can locate the elements of Pound's "theory" of translation deep in the vaults of literary history.

We all know that Cicero and Horace warned against word-for-word translation, just as we know that Augustine and Boethius warned against taking advice on these matters from the likes of Cicero and Horace.[10] We all know it because it is the kind of easy categorical thinking that tends to stick in the mind: the free or the literal, just that simple. Unfortunately, it does little to reveal to us just how the translator sees his task or his text. Catullus says that he "imitates" or "expresses" ("expressa . . . carmina") Callimachus in his version of the *Coma Berenices,* and we can only get a sense of the complex intention that verb implies by looking at both the "close" *Coma* and the more restive Sappho 31. Quintilian moves to a new level of secondary insight with this, from *De institutione oratoria* 10.5.4: "Neque ego paraphrasin esse interpretationem tantum volo, sed circa eosdem sensus certamen atque aemulationem."[11] We will never understand all the sentence implies, never quite be sure of the proper balance of "certamen" and "aemulatio," even while we *are* sure that Quintilian is onto something. One can see that "certamen," a kind of rivalry, is near the heart of Catullus 51, although it is far from the spirit of his Callimachus. Kelly (1979, 60–63) polarizes the predispositions of translators into two camps: those who observe the "friendship" model, the sharing of goals and insight, almost an intimacy (a notion given most vivid theoretical life by Roscommon) and those who subscribe to Quintilian's "competition," the desire to adapt a text, even improve it. Augustine, Boethius, Dryden, Campbell, Letourner, Shelley, and Day Lewis among others are seen to observe the first model, Cicero, Jerome, the medieval humanists, Cowley, Pope, Herder, and others, the second. Such models, as Kelly would agree, do little justice to a translator's quite complex intention, but they do begin to lead us to a deeper understanding. One of them strikes something in Pound; note the language of personal relation:

> Catullus, Propertius, Horace, and Ovid are the people who matter . . .
> Propertius for his beautiful cadence though he uses only one meter . . .
> Vergil is a second-rater.

> I shall have to read a few Latin and Greek things aloud to you [Iris Barry], and possibly try to translate 'em. The value being that the Roman poets are the only ones we know of who had approximately the same problems we have. (*Letters,* 138 and 141)

Patently, and this has not been noticed often enough, Pound is proposing a model of thinking about and translating certain classical poets that is phrased in personal terms and based in cooperation, even collaboration. Further, the translator's job of work is to bring some *personal* essence, more than a verbal presence, into modern English and to people now. This is a notion shared by many translators, but for Pound it may go yet deeper given his conspicuous and explicit use of Cavalcanti, Daniel, and Li Po as "personae," personal masks, tentative identities.[12] The connection between author and translator can penetrate to the deepest levels of being and consciousness. Stephen MacKenna, the Plotinus translator who shared some of Pound's amateurism—and his accomplishment—gets nearest to expressing this intimacy.

> Whenever I look into Plotinus I feel always all the old trembling fevered longing: it seems to me that I must be born for him, and that somehow

someday I must have nobly translated him: my heart, untravelled, still
to Plotinus turns and drags at each remove a lengthening chain. It seems
to me that him alone of authors I understand by inborn sight. . . .[13]

That Pound seems to have had something of the same feeling for Propertius is
betrayed by his praise, surprising to some scholars, of the Roman's "cadence" (a word near Pound's poetic heart) and his independence from
political jingoism—beauties colored, at least in part, by the eye of the
beholder. The deeply rooted affinity between writers is important; a key to
the poem's force is surely the freshly compounded yet single voice, even
sympathy, Pound and Propertius tentatively share in the *Homage.*
    Bearing upon this image of translation is another equally ancient trans-
lator's guide: didacticism.

> I am perhaps didactic: so in a sense, or in different senses are Homer,
> Dante, Villon, and Omar, and Fitzgerald's translation of Omar is the
> only good poem of the Victorian era that has got beyond a fame de
> cenacle. It's all rubbish to pretend that art isn't didactic. A revelation is
> always didactic. Only the aesthetes since 1880 have pretended the
> contrary, and they weren't a very sturdy lot. (*Letters,* 248)

Opposed to the didactic element in translation are any number of translators, beginning perhaps with Cicero, who have taken a source text as a
pretext for new poetic enrichment and accomplishment. The source text
matters less than what can be done with it; transmission becomes secondary
to creation. But, as Kelly writes (1979, 47–48), Pound, for all his exercise of
creative energies in translation, focuses in his intent primarily upon what
Herder called *Erklärung.* The translator, in Pound's view, is a mediator of an
entire complex of experience and revelations represented by the original text,
the reader's capacity to understand which Pound never overestimates. He
remains intensely loyal to the legacy he would transmit. On Cavalcanti:

> I have in my translations tried to bring over the qualities of Guido's
> rhythm, not line for line, but to embody in the whole of my English
> some trace of that power which implies the man. The science of the
> music of words, and the knowledge of their magical powers has fallen
> away since men invoked Mithra by a sequence of pure vowel sounds.
> That there might be less interposed between the reader and Guido, it
> was my first intention to print only his poem and an unrhymed gloze.
> This has not been practicable. I cannot trust the reader to read the
> Italian for the music after he has read the English for the sense. (*Transla-
> tions,* 24)

Pound's didacticism must then, involve selection, the application of magisterial judgment to point out to a less expert audience precisely what most

needs to be transmitted. All the usual pedagogical techniques can be expected: exaggeration of important features, omission of the less crucial, summary, dramatic flair, argument. And these are features prominent in the *Homage:* "I certainly omitted no means that I saw open to me, including shortenings, cross-cuts, implications derivable from other writings of Propertius. . ." (*Letters*, 311). All this suggests an almost hyperactive inquisition of the text, a flurry of critical energy to get at some central meaning that is not only the "truth" but the "hidden truth." That , in turn, may be part of a larger and chronic pattern of discovery in Pound noted by Sanford Schwartz: "The modern 'seeker after knowledge' must therefore view the past with a critical eye; he must delve beneath official history and search for traces of alternative values that have been ideologically distorted and physically suppressed."[14] Searching for that kind of truth is bound to stir up reaction and resentment, even when the seeker sets out in innocence and curiosity and returns, as Pound did, fully convinced of the validity of his insight. Thus, although shaken by salvos of criticism, the mission of teaching, of giving over the truest essence of Propertius, remains the unshakable and unabashed center of the poem. "I shall be quite content if I induce a few Latinists really to look at the text of Propertius instead of swallowing an official 'position' and then finding what the textbooks tell them to look for" (*Letters*, 311). *Magister* to the end.

But there *is* a rub. Pound's model for translation seems to be that of personal trust between author and translator. At stake in such a situation, as Hugh Kenner points out, are not "words" but "essences": "the rendering, without deformation, of something, within him or without, which he has clearly apprehended and seized in his mind . . . a rendering of a mode of thought or feeling. . . . He does not translate the words. The words have led him to the thing he expresses" (*Translations*, 10–11). The translator distinguishes, in Pound's words, between "wot a man sez and wot he means." But such absolute diffraction of an author's light through a translator's mind—without the guiding orientation of the words—leaves little tangible evidence of connection, for its readers, between the original poem and translation. What from Pound's view are perfectly evident principles of conversion can be to most readers opaque. Pedagogical techniques of selection, omission, emphasis are seen to be tendentious argument. *Erklärung* shades into impressionism; illustration becomes creative redirection; and translation, appropriation. All this is particularly true when the authentic commitment to an author's "essence"—his "rhythm," "mental content," and material context—must be translated through another poet's powerfully creative imagination.

It is the reader's exclusion, his inability to understand Pound's motives, commitments, methods, that accounts for many of the "flaws" critics have discovered in the *Homage.* Similarly, Pound's failure was his indifference to making clear the logic of relation between Propertius's voice and his own. To this extent the poem did not succeed as translation, and Pound seems to have known it. His surprise at the adverse criticism, his defensiveness, convey both his hopes for comprehension from his readers and his sense of failure. And so, retraction. "If the reader does not find relation to life defined in the poem, he may conclude that I have been unsuccessful in my endeavor" (*Letters*, 311). "No, I have not done a translation." He chose finally to claim only that he was presenting "certain emotions" vital to Propertius and to us. It is a remarkable falling back. But what I have tried to show, in part, is that such retraction does not, in the objective light of this later day, make the poem any less a translation than it ever was. It is still "a poem [for] which a poem in another language . . . is the vitalizing, shaping presence; a poem which can be read and responded to independently, but which is not on-tologically complete. . . ." (Steiner 1966, 34). More specifically, Pound's *Homage* need not be seen as a "free fantasy" or dominated by a perverse creativity. On the contrary, it seems to be firmly anchored in common models and motives of translation that seek to preserve fidelity to some perceived essence and to communicate that sense to its readers. His retrac-tion suggests no more than his failure to communicate to others just what he was about.

* * *

Up to this point, discussion has been general, so as to locate and sketch out Pound's largest assumptions and intentions in making the translation he did. It is a necessary preliminary to more specific treatment insofar as it adumbrates certain goals, a framework of general intent to be fleshed out by technique and specific stylistic decision.

Four lines—some limited ground for technique and decision:

> Callimachi manes et Coi sacra Philetae
>   in vestrum, quaeso, me sinite ire nemus
> primus ego ingredior puro de fonte sacerdos
>   Itala per Graios orgia ferre choros.

So begins the well-known program poem (4.1 in Mueller—Pound's Teubner, 3.1 and 3.2 in modern editions). Propertius is signaling his fidelity to the objectives and styles of his two most prominent Alexandrian precursors. The mere mention of these names to the small, educated Roman audience the poems were intended for calls forth a full complex of ideas, aesthetic prefer-ences, and associations. But, clearly, a modern audience—one likely to be reading a translation—will have trouble understanding just what is signified by these two strange names, Callimachus and Philetas. A similar problem is presented by "puro de fonte" or any of a dozen other stock phrases, topoi, and figures, all of which function synecdochically, suggesting more than they say. Obviously, to understand the proper shading of meaning of "exactus tenui pumice versus eat" (l. 8), the tension between its formulaic commonness (compare Catullus 1) and the exclusivity and individuality it points to, one must know more than simply "the Latin." If one considers the needs of the modern audience, then, translating words, as Kenner says, won't do. But what will? If the problem is to call forth the full range of reference and understanding implicit in the Latin with a few English words bound loosely to the original, one must from the start concede failure. "The impossibility of translation" is of course one of our oldest and most common ideas. Augustine and Roger Bacon made much of it and the notion has persisted until now in a variety of forms through Carne-Ross, Quine, and others. But if one evasively skirts the thorny theoretical issue and pragmatically abandons hope for a "total multidimensional translation" settling for something more modest, say, (in Kelly's words) "to find in the translation the same equilibrium between *signifié, signifiant,* and human user as in the original text," or to preserve Steiner's "conservation of the energies of meaning," a degree of achievement remains within reach.

Pound's attempt to present an "equilibrium" between text and reader similar to that between the elegy and its reader requires a shifting of frames of reference. Pound, then, presumes an audience that is not intimate with the details of Callimachean aesthetics, with formula and topos, or with Propertius's subtly antagonistic attitude toward Horace (whom he quotes many times in this poem in barbed imitation). And on. Instead of depending upon such understandings, he must look to others: what a reasonably literate common reader knows about contemporary poetry, particularly the "cadences" of Pound's new and natural free verse as distinguished from the rhythms and tired diction of Victorian and Edwardian translationese; what makes up a modern "ironic tone"; how one might express fierce dedication to his art while depreciating "the idiocies of one's predecessors"; what composes a contemporary political and social frame of reference most analogous to Propertius's. This in mind, he begins.

> Shades of Callimachus, Coan ghosts of Philetas,
> It is in your grove I would walk,
> I who came first from the clear font
> Bringing the Grecian orgies into Italy, and the dance into Italy.

His first line, as first lines often do, has attracted attention. We are told that it is one of Pound's many mistranslations. So G. M. Messing as late as 1975:

> Let me now turn to erroneous collocations of words. To begin at the very beginning, there is "Coan ghosts of Philetas" for "Coi sacra Philetae" (3.1.1). Sullivan is convinced that "the line succeeds rhyth-

mically and the meaning is not changed" but he is noticeably uneasy about Richardson's flashier defense of it. The latter argues that retention of the Latin word order is itself a desideratum, surely a claim without foundation, even if Pound himself believed it. In an inflected language like Latin a freer word order is permitted than in an analytic language like English. The illusory goal of copying a Latinate word order in English can appeal only to pseudo-linguists, like the Fenellosa theories about copying Chinese structure in English. "Coan ghosts of Philetas" is a long way from "the rites of Philetas of Cos."[15]

The essential problem with this censure is that the accusations do not quite strike home. In spite of Richardson's appreciative hypothesis, Pound can never have intended simply to "copy Latinate word order." Here is Pound's criticism of Milton from 1916: "He tried to turn English into Latin; to use an uninflected language as if it were an inflected one, neglecting the genius of English, distorting its fibrous manner, making schoolboy translations of Latin phrases: 'Him who disobeys me disobeys' " ("Notes," 109). And this, of Browning's *Agamemnon*, sometime before 1918: "What Browning had not got into his sometimes excellent top-knot was the patent, or what should be the patent fact, that inversions of sentence order in an uninflected language like English are not, simply and utterly *are not* any sort of equivalent for inversions and perturbations of order in a language inflected as Greek and Latin are inflected" ("Translators," 148). Clearly Pound did not "believe" what Messing presumes him to have believed. The line reads as it does for other reasons; it does "succeed rhythmically" as Sullivan maintains, but also makes better sense than Messing's literal version—granting, of course, that the scholar is not trying to write poetry. Messing would preserve the Latin syntax; Pound transfers an epithet—always a conventional and usually an unobjectionable procedure—to make a neater parallel in English. Further, Messing would translate "sacra" as "rites" (its ordinary sense), which presents problems in this case. A. E. Housman has pointed out the logical difficulty "in appealing to both 'rites' and 'spirits' for permission to enter" the grove. The difficulty might be alleviated for classicists by D. R. Shackleton Bailey's contention that "manes et sacra" was a stereotyped expression and Propertius probably used it (both words applying to both poets) without close analysis, but it remains thorny for translators who have to make clearer sense in English. A help is Lawrence Richardson and Shackleton Bailey (provisionally) who suppose that "sacra" might be taken as "ashes" or "relics," while John P. Postgate provides further guidance in proposing that "sacra" is virtually synonymous with "manes." Pound, obviously not following Postgate but his own sense of balance and propriety, has taken this last course, incidentally eliminating what would be for the modern reader extraneous ritual and sacral connotations. Pound's is quite evidently a translator's choice that provides clear resolution to a textual difficulty where Messing's reading does not.

The point of dwelling just a bit on one scholar's criticisms here is to show that his asking "how well did Pound know his Latin?" (although it is a perfectly valid question[16]) is perhaps not the best tactic to take if one wants either to understand what the English is getting at or to evaluate its success as translation, insofar as that translation involves so much more or other than locating and transmitting "right sense"—something more elusive and difficult than we might at first assume. In Nida's terms, strictures of formal correspondence applied to a methodology based in dynamic equivalence serve no good end.[17]

But to cover quickly the first few lines, what else does Pound do? His second line comes close to the Latin in sense but adopts a more commanding tone—"I would" replacing "quaeso, me sinite." The third employs a relative, "who," which is not there in the Latin but which serves to link the thoughts of the first four lines appropriately. "Sacerdos" is dropped, perhaps because of a Horatian tincture to the word—Pound making more explicit, possibly, the two poets' antipathy. More likely is another shift in establishing dynamic equivalence: the modern(-ist) poet has lost all sacerdotal coloring; why then call him "priest"? Hitherto, Pound's translation has been of a recognizable kind and its guiding principles clear: bearing his modern non-classical audience in mind, Pound works toward clarity in a decidedly English poetic idiom, attempting to present something analogous to the poetic experience of Propertius's own readers. What, then, of line 4?

> Itala per Graios orgia ferre choros
>
> Bringing the Grecian orgies into Italy, and the dance into Italy.

Critics of this obviously inexact translation want to locate here the pattern of Pound's many divergencies from the Latin: can Pound have entirely misconstrued the phrase, believing that "Graios orgia," both words being accusative, must go together; that "choros" must be another object; and that "per" governs "Itala"? And finally, can he have mistranslated "orgia," which most literally indicates ceremonial Bacchic "revels," as "orgies"? It is, however, hardly possible to believe that Pound thought his a literal translation; to do so would be to fall into the word-order trap he so often and so vehemently warned against. Pound knew the principles of case and gender agreement. So what did he intend? Richardson and Sullivan propose the "collage of sense" model, "which consists in taking a few of the Latin words, ignoring their grammatical connections and offering for their original meaning an impressionistic sentence which fits plausibly into what has gone before" (Sullivan 1964, 100). That makes sense without quite fully explaining intention or result. The "collage" model does, however, point to an element of play that is doubtless active in the *Homage*. We see it in the frequent puns ("rigavit" as "stiffen," "canes" as "dogs"), in the bits of anachronism (Hesiod as "Wordsworthian"), and—if Sullivan is correct—in the whole "logopoeic" texture of the verse. But in addition to the play, informing it, is something more complicated and purposeful.

In this case ("Bringing the Grecian orgies into Italy"), Pound's "aggressive" misprision[18] lies not so much in his breaking up the Latin syntax but in his interpretation of the line's most central importance. Propertius's claim that he is first to bring Greek forms to Latin material is a peculiarly Roman notion of originality. For the English reader, originality lies in other kinds of factors, the "genius" that transcends convention, say. To complicate the matter, Propertius followed Horace in precisely this claim and in practice was preceded by at least Catullus (and quite probably others of the neoterics as well). Propertius's claim to originality, then, rendered *ad verbum,* could hardly be appreciated by a modern audience and must be recast. Pound's lines do so by inverting the significances of the Latin words: the discipline and form of "Graios choros" is replaced by something suiting a more modern sense of poetic creativity, "Grecian orgies," (cf. the Yeatsian "dance"). "Italian," having lost its "orgia" becomes nominalized, "Italy," and inert—much like Pound's vision of postwar England—hence requiring the charge of new idea. Propertius's originality, via Pound, loses all its conventional aspects, becomes precisely unconventional, and (this is Pound's "restitution") invigorates tired poetic routine. The *almost* awkward repeats of "into Italy" and the ungainliness of the long line indicate an initial difficulty, an adjustment, that is resolved, then, in a more naturalized and easy restatement: "the dance into Italy." It is an anatomizing of the process of bringing Propertius—as new idea—into English. Propertius's creative accomplishment is effected by his manipulation, subtle twisting, of a number of conventions—the restricted codes of the Latin love elegy—that don't exist in English verse; Pound's translation of that accomplishment, then, requires both aggressive appropriation and restitution (in the language of Steiner) in terms indigenous to the modern poetic *Zeitgeist*.

We have dwelt, perhaps inordinately, on these introductory lines to a purpose. First, to show some of the difficulties resident in translating a poem so distant in time and perspective; a sea change in form and in the accidents of expression is required. Second, to demonstrate a consistent intellectual method in Pound, which attempts to render the crucial germ of Propertius's presence in modern idiom (although often enough not in a pure "modern English"). He will not render what everyone sees in Propertius and so, for some, will fail, as Pound himself contended. But it is distracting and unproductive to dwell upon "error" as merely that in Pound's translation—as I hope these few lines have shown—and much more to the mark to notice his most characteristic "patterns of conversion" and evaluate their success in accomplishing what they set out to do.

Yet, dismissing the general preoccupation with Pound's "mistakes" is a little too easy. They are demonstrably compelling—a fact only partially explained by the critic's need to show how much more he knows than the poet does. The poem itself is more responsible. It is not coy or modest or humble. It is brash as it seems to turn away from the Latin: "We have kept our erasers in order," "celebrities from the trans-Caucasus will belaud Roman celebrities," "equipped with a frigidaire patent," "Jove in East Elis," "stiffened our faces with the backwash of Philetas the Coan," "night dogs, the marks of a drunken scurry." Critics are naturally drawn to such audacious re-presentations, and even general readers (who ordinarily have the better sense) too often, as Sullivan laments, read the poem only for its sensational lines. If the poem did not seem to some to be so flamboyantly careless, more of us might have given its individual sections the attention they deserve—so, too, if we did not hear Pound say through the very rubric of the poem, "There is Propertius and here am I." What comes between the two, their logic of relation, is precisely and naturally what in the literal sense "interests."

And so in what remains of this discussion our focus will fall often enough upon Pound's apparent divergences from the Propertian text. But not with exclusive intent. They are most interesting not in themselves but as elements of larger movements of the translator's purpose. Those movements, the rhythms of mind, can be traced. At the most elementary level of understanding, they oscillate between the poles of literalness and freedom, and it would seem both efficient and logical to begin at that crude perception. Let us examine, then, two apparently contrasting sections of the poem, one very "close," one less so, both to compare their translational mechanics and to estimate their relative consistency.

*   *   *

Not all of the *Homage* is condemned by its hostile critics. Messing, for instance, approving heartily of section 3, calls it "brilliantly successful." It is easy enough to see why. It begins:

> Midnight, and a letter comes to me from our mistress:

For:

> nox media, et dominae mihi venit epistula nostrae.

This is very close translation, right down to the overly literal "our," and the rest of the section follows suit. Its variances from the Latin are unobtrusive and of a consistent tonal piece. We are not confused by this translation; we can follow the reason of its wanderings. There are few mythological allusions to get wrong and no political drum to beat into anti-Augustan or anti-imperial-British noise. The English is simple, and at points lovely.

> Midnight, and a letter comes to me from our mistress:
>   Telling me to come to Tibur, *At* once!!
> "Bright tips reach up from twin towers,
>   Anienan spring water falls into flat-spread pools."

This translation fits neatly into our customary expectations. Little wonder, then, that many should approve, yet this approbation is founded on the least tenable of grounds. Unobtrusiveness, an unwillingness to disturb conventional expectations, has seldom been held, per se, as a valid principle of translation. The formal correspondences of Benjamin's theorizing and Browning's practice radically disturb English syntax. The far broader range of dynamic equivalences are based at root on the notion of some necessary disturbance of source language patterns. So, rather than rely on grounds so tenuous for their praise and blame, critics of the *Homage* most often fall back upon the argument that Pound's more outrageous translations violate the "flavour" or "spirit" of Propertius: "Such renderings pervert the flavour of a consciously artistic, almost academic, original"; "Something more fundamental, a violation of the spirit of Propertius is at stake. Pound has forced the tone."[19] Presumably, section 3 does not violate such "spirit" and so "succeeds."

But what is this spirit of Propertius?

> nox media, et dominae mihi venit epistula nostrae:
>   Tibure me missa iussit adesse mora,
> candida qua geminas ostendunt culmina turres,
>   et cadit in patulos lympha Aniena lacus.
> quid faciam? obductis commitam mene tenebris,
>   ut timeam audaces in mea membra manus?
> at si distulero haec nostro mandata timore,
>   nocturno fletus saevior hoste mihi.
> peccaram semel, et totum sum postus in annum:
>   in me mansuetas non habet illa manus.
> nec tamen est quisquam, sacros qui laedat amantes:
>   Scironis media sic licet ire via.
> quisquis amator erit, Scythicis licet ambulet oris:
>   nemo adeo ut noceat barbarus esse volet.
> luna ministrat iter, demonstrant astra salebras,
>   ipse Amor accensas percutit ante faces,
> saeva canum rabies morsus avertit hiantis:
>   huic generi quovis tempore tuta viast.

sanguine tam parvo quis enim spargatur amantis
    inprobus? ecce, suis fit comes ipsa Venus.
quod si certa meos sequerentur funera casus,
    talis mors pretio vel sit emenda mihi.
adferet haec unguenta mihi sertisque sepulcrum
    ornabit custos ad mea busta sedens.
di faciant, mea ne terra locet ossa frequenti,
    qua facit adsiduo tramite volgus iter!
post mortem tumuli sic infamantur amantum:
    me tegat arborea devia terra coma,
aut humer ignotae cumulis vallatus harenae:
    non iuvat in media nomen habere via.

                                3.16 (4.15 Mueller)

Midnight, a lover's note demands his presence; he wants to go, but is it safe to travel at this hour? This barest of themes provides Propertius the opportunity to run skillfully through the major topoi of the subjective love elegy: the active, demanding female and the passive, hopelessly addicted male; the privileged, almost sacrosanct position of the lover over against the hostile, vulgar world; the intervention of Venus and Cupid on a lover's behalf that does little to alleviate a final hopelessness. Beyond these elements, the typically Propertian preoccupation with death finds a place here and though formulaic in this instance, lends an edge of psychological pressure to the verse not found in the other elegists. Furthermore, and again typically, Propertius manages these utterly conventional subjects to ambivalent effect: self-ironic wit on the one hand and intense emotional exhibitionism on the other. Ovid never comes near to such a subtle balance and Catullus only rarely. Above all, there is nothing affected about this performance; Propertius's voice leans toward urgency and away from complacency. For all his fear and passivity, this Propertius is not emasculated; the poem's tensions could not work if he were.

Yet an emasculated voice is precisely what Pound's translation most prominently exhibits.

> What *is* to be done about it?
>   Shall I entrust myself to entangled shadows,
> Where bold hands may do violence to my person?
>
> Yet if I postpone my obedience
>   because of this respectable terror
> I shall be prey to lamentations worse than a nocturnal
>   assailant.
>
> *And* I shall be in the wrong,
> *And* it will last a twelve month,
> For her hands have no kindness me-ward. . . .

The tone is effete, the diction stilted. This language ("where bold hands may do violence to my person . . . this respectable terror . . . no kindness me-ward") recalls the precious locutions of Prufrock. Moreover, this voice has none of the equally delicate Mauberley's compensations; the single lovely Poundian image in the poem is quoted (in Pound's version) from Cynthia's "note"":

> "Bright tips reach up from twin towers
> Anienan spring water falls into flat-spread pools."

It is not unnatural for Propertius's speaker to use language like this, but Pound's persona, at least here, cannot. He hasn't the gumption or the ear. The fastidious, affected tone is consistent: "No barbarism would go to the extent of doing him harm . . . the stars will point out the stumbles . . . who is so indecorous as to shed the pure gore of a suitor?! / Cypris is his cicerone . . . God's aid, let not my bones lie in a public location / with crowds too assiduous in their crossing of it . . . or may I inter beneath the hummock / of some as yet uncatalogued sand; / at any rate I shall not have my epitaph on the high road." When Propertius writes, "sanguine tam parvo quis enim spargatur amantis," he indicates the delicate and fragile figure the lover presents to a harder world, yet for the Latin poet the psychological fires burn with a compensating ferocity. Pound's lover shows little, none, of the burning, only the dandified surface of Eliot's Prufrock, the self-possessed and self-conscious inadequacy of the speaker in "Portrait of A Lady":

> I take my hat: how can I make cowardly amends
> For what she has said to me?

From one view, then, Pound's departure from the "spirit" of Propertius is radical, even when the techniques of translation are undemonstrative. By this criterion, according to the critics, the translation fails. But of course Messing and others are perfectly correct in finding section 3 precisely *not* a failure. Pound has passed over much of what Propertius offers, but what he does take across the frontiers of language becomes a poem of marvelous wit and integrity. Moreover, it suits its time. He has taken over the voice nearest to Propertius's Alexandrianism, the refined "aesthetic" sophistication that dominates verse and fiction from the decadents through Eliot, Huxley, and Waugh. The dynamic equivalence is apt in spite of its failure to bring across all the complications of Propertius's tenor; the words of the poem are natural to this speaker, and the modern reader, in spite of the unfamiliar topoi, understands perfectly their significances and ambiance. The case seems to present a classic demonstration of Steiner's hermeneutic motion: trust, aggression, incorporation, restitution.[20] The crucial point of interpretive action comes in the "aggression" phase when Pound must ruthlessly select from the potential significances of the source text. The salient germ of the original he chooses to develop is self-reflexive irony. He then incorporates that irony into a modern mode—contemporary language in a contemporary character—and next restores or compensates for what he has selected out by development and enrichment of his chosen theme. The point is finally that any "classic" text, or any text worth translating for artistic purposes (so Steiner's "trust"), involves (in the language of Levi-Strauss through Kermode[21]) a plurality of significances a great many of which cannot survive translation. However disappointing, this state of affairs is precisely analogous to that of interpretation in general which at any point in history will give only a partial view of a text's potential meaning. So Propertius is necessarily more inclusive, more "plural," than any of Pound's (or any other translator's) versions. He suggests the character Pound develops in section 3, but complicates it with contrastive dimensions of personality and art. That particular complex works for a Roman audience and, to a lesser extent, for classicists. It does not work for a modern translator's audience, the general reader acquainted with contemporary poetry; hence the choices Pound makes and the compensations he provides.

All this bears on one or two large issues. First, the question already raised of an original author's sacrosanct "spirit," which Pound is so often presumed to violate. It is an empty criterion. "Spirit," even if it were objectively describable, must involve the full complex of the poet's art, his complete signifying potential. Such totality, never accessible to any translator or interpreter at any particular time, is always to some degree traduced by the *traduttore*. Nevertheless it is possible to "traduce" faithfully, to engage and "restore" a text while remaining immensely loyal to the element of its art perceived as most crucial, most essential. Pound, the paradigmatic modern, naturally finds a modernized Propertius and artfully communicates that to his contemporary readers. The essence of what Pound does in translating, then, resides not in reproducing (or failing to reproduce) "spirit," nor in faithfulness to Propertius's words or the accidents of his mythological and geographical references, nor in the relative degree of the translation's own creative obtrusiveness, its flamboyance of diction and style—all of which are most commonly cited or criticized in the *Homage*. Rather it resides in the artistic integrity of its hermeneutic motion, of the discernible movement of intellect from a tactful interpretation to a text of full poetic unity, of adequate verbal resource and significance. Again, the result is not "independent" poetry but is bound to the original as by an act of faith: this vision of Propertius is Pound's idea of the irreducible center of the Latin, a necessarily partial vision that flowers under a master's hand into an English counterpart of near-equal accomplishment. Pound's translation is then an act of intellectual passage where the distance between original and rendering is a measure of the compensatory gain Pound shores up against the initial and obvious loss a translation must suffer.

Nearly all of Pound's alterations and most of his so-called errors can be seen in this light. When Pound omits the adverb in "candida qua geminas ostendunt culmina turres" so that he may "present" the plain image, "Bright tips reaching up from twin towers," he draws directly from the technical repertoire of modern poetics to augment and enrich the translator's partial vision. The method is consistent right on through the section's final line, "at any rate I shall not have my epitaph in a high road," uttered, we sense, with a bored and fastidious sigh—a version of Propertius enriched with a personality and sense of character, a full and rounded dimensionality of voice. This kind of compensatory enrichment is precisely an "homage," an homage to the more complete poetic achievement it attempts, using its own means, to approach.

*   *   *

An interesting locus for comparison to the seemingly close translation of *Homage* 3 is the last section (12) of the poem where the *New Age* reviewer finds "seven major blunders" among many more minor slips. It is freer in its manner of expression, more selective in choosing what it wants to translate, and well stocked with famous Poundian additions, e.g., "Vergil is Phoebus' chief of police." This caprice is made more interesting in light of the fact that section 12 translates a single poem (2.32 in Mueller, 2.34 in modern texts) rather than accreting bits and pieces from several as he does in his other "freer" sections—6, 10, and 11 conspicuously. Perhaps the most obviously disturbing elements of this translation are its omissions. From a poem of ninety-four or so lines, twenty-seven are completely dropped and many others minimally accounted for. An additional complicating factor is the nature of the original, a poem that has caused textual and literary critics numerous difficulties. While this is not the place to rehearse all the problems the text presents, we can simply note that the poem is patently not a well-integrated whole. Barth first, and others later, divided the poem into two parts (1–24 and 25–44). The first section, if we call it that, focuses on a romantic rivalry. Lynceus, ostensibly a friend, has made overtures to Propertius's Cynthia, apparently after becoming intoxicated at a party. The theme is friendship's fragility when a woman comes between, and the lines are full of jealous indignation and passionate rhetoric. The next section (through 1.64), however, takes an entirely different tone, that of the "magister amoris," as it describes the inadequacy of Lyncaeus's "serious" poetic background for successful amatory verse and outlines the changes he will have to make. An aside praising Vergil's achievement comes next and finally a list of the poets Propertius most admires, the love poets, culminating (or ending) with himself. Seen as a single poem, its effect is confusing; the tone clearly shifts several times and does so inexplicably. One could say, with Richardson and others, that it is an unsatisfactory work. Why, then, should Pound have chosen this piece to crown his translation?

At least in part the answer is the poem's very inconsistency. Pound may have seen an opportunity to put some kind of resolution to Propertius' persistently troubling elusiveness, his refusal to be pinned down. The poem presents ample opportunity for exercising such an ambition. Another answer is the work's range. It begins with what most people have considered to be the "essential" Propertius, the love poet, but moves in quick fashion through most of his major themes: the implicit *recusatio*, the (possibly) ironic praise of Vergil's Augustanism, the poetic "choice of life," and finally and most important for Pound, the full and unequivocal dedication to a certain kind of art. Pound seems to have considered the progress of these themes, their sequence, important as a record of Propertius's attachments, and the priorities that seem to emerge from the poem suit the modernist very well. Thus, if any poem could be said to "summarize" Propertius, 2.34 may do it best.

The character of Pound's initial translating act, his interpretive "aggression," can be discerned from what Pound leaves out of the first twenty-four lines:

> sic erepta mihi paene puella meast.   (2)

> Lynceu, tune meam potuisti, perfide, curam
>   tangere? nonne tuae tum cecidere manus? (9–10)

> ipse meas solus, quod nil est, aemulor umbras,
>   stultus, quod nullo saepe timore tremo.
> una tamen causast, cur crimina tanta remitto. (19–21)

The first section is the most immediately confessional of the whole poem, and it is easy to see what effect the elimination of lines like this has on a translation. Lines 19–20 are particularly strong, "I am jealous of even my own shadow," and only overriding belief that the heart of the poem lies elsewhere could justify its omission. In demonstrating such a belief, Pound has allowed the first few lines he does translate to dominate the tenor of the entire section:

> cur quisquam faciem dominae iam credit amico? . . .
> expertus dico, nemost in amore fidelis:
>   formosam raro non sibi quisque petit.
> polluit ille deus cognatos, solvit amicos,
>   et bene concordes tristia ad arma vocat.
> Tros et in hospitium Menelao venit adulter
>   Colchis et ignotum nonne secuta virumst?

This, in isolation, is utterly impersonal. Even "expertus dico" is lifeless and tired. Pound takes the hint:

> Who will be the next man to entrust his girl to a friend?
> Love interferes with fidelities;
> The gods have brought shame on their relatives;
>   Each man wants the pomegranate for himself;
> Amiable and harmonious people are pushed incontinent into
>   duels,
> A Trojan and adulterous person came to Menelaus under the rites
>   of hospitium,
> And there was a case in Colchis, Jason and that woman in
>   Colchis;

Pound takes the plausible view that Propertius's jealousy is merely conventional, that there is nothing of real personal involvement in it. Even the ostensibly strong "Lynceu, tune meam potuisti, perfide, curam / tangere?" and sentiments like it *might* be seen as stock protestations. In part, this tone reflects Pound's own lack of interest in the amatory idiom, but the ease with which Propertius seems to shift into his "real" subject in 25–94 lends support to Pound's opinion. Certainly the magisterial voice evident later in the Latin is exaggerated in the early parts of the translation. But here is a jaded "magister," fatigued, not rejuvenated, by his huge amorous experience. Pound gives us a Byronic Propertius, absently running through once again the long-memorized motions of love's rhetoric. Pound's every phrase is discrete, virtually unrelated to the next, as if the emotion that might have bound them together has run its course. Feeble efforts at playful variation, the Don Juan's last resort, evident in the diction—"pomegranate" and "able and harmonious people"—betray the boredom that motivates them. It is perhaps more interesting that the tone of ennui and stupefying inertia is present not only in the language and phrasing Pound uses, but even in the very *process* of his translation—as if the jaded persona Pound infers from the text were itself translating the poem. "Polluit ille deus cognatos, solvit amicos" becomes almost nonsensically, "The gods have brought shame on their relatives." Casual, disinterested paraphrase, too unconcerned to quibble about singular-plural distinctions, plausible sense, or accounting for all the words. The same can be said for "A Trojan and adulterous person" and the entire line "And there was a case in Colchis, Jason and that woman in Colchis" (for "Colchis et ignotum nonne secuta virumst?"), whose stylistic clumsiness demonstrates a voice so sated with the habits of mythological allusion that it has simply ceased to care.

This apparent intrusion of a persona's voice and manner into the very act of translation is a remarkable innovation that accounts for many of the imprecisions critics have noticed in this section. G. T. Wright (1960, 136) was the first to suggest the notion:

> The persona becomes, in the first instance, the ancient speaker; in the second, the speaker augmented by the new poet's sense of him; and, in the third, both these faces, taking their place in the larger textual unit of which they are a part, and ultimately in the whole poem.[22]

That is an astute analysis and gets quite near to it. Yet we have something more here than Pound and Propertius interfused, passively there, as text; rather we have a *tertium quid,* for convenience called a persona, that represents the sum of Pound's "trust" (that core of Propertius which comes through) and his aggressive interpretation, actively there, a demanding and motivating presence that actually dictates the direction the ongoing translation takes. It can so dictate because this persona functions, almost like a *daimon* of myth, as a mediator. More than sharing features of both poems or poets, it keeps them in a kind of artificial yet exuberant copresence. The interstices of these two poetic worlds, the margins of their intercourse, become unstable, unpredictable, under the pressure of Pound's *act* of translation. Now one, now the other voice, emerging from not only the respective poetic texts but from the larger semiotic—literary and cultural—systems that engender them, seems to take precedence. We see a mobile play of language oscillating between poles of sensibility, but not randomly, instead disciplined by a purposeful compounded intelligence. Cavalier misprisions such as "head farmers do likewise, and lying weary among their oats" and "like a trained and performing tortoise" are more satisfactorily resolved by this than by any other explanation. It is an audacious technical device since quite naturally it leaves the translator open to charges of incompetence—the line between that and intended casualness being difficult indeed to discern.

That Pound was aware of what he was doing and tried to point it out to critics without giving too much of the game away is evident from his letter to the *New Age:* "I think it as likely that Mount Cythaeron played the lute as that the walls of Thebes rose to the magic of Amphion's solo on the barbitos. Also I am tired, very tired, of Amphion and of lyres, whether of tortoise shell or some less brittle compost . . . these emotions are given largely, but not entirely, in Propertius's own terms" (*Letters,* 179). The boredom with stock mythological allusions is clearly something Pound himself felt, but there is a compounding of the feeling in his translation's persona, and it is the sentiment of the latter, i.e., his own poetic intent colored by the demands he sees in the translated text, which governs the technical and tonal choices the translation makes in the later stages of its process. The implications of this novel situation are (within the small world of translation study) startling. Relations between the two languages become more complicated, and an element of control is abandoned. Pound translates as he feels Propertius might have translated ("largely . . . in Propertius's own terms"), or at least as this inferred vision of the Latin poet might have done. Immediately the varied implications of the "friendship" model of translation come to mind— the personified original text, the element of personal relation between the two authors, the fidelity to what the translator perceives as the original's most crucial essence augmented, enriched, as in section 3, by compensatory gains that are somehow appropriate to ancient poet and modern circumstance. So, too, the "possession" of the translator by the original author so vividly described by MacKenna: ". . . it seems to me that I must be born for him." Critics are fond of claiming that Pound appropriates Propertius. In fact the opposite is nearer the truth. Some of the poem's most remarkable lines derive precisely from what amounts to an abandonment of authorial control in favor of what this vision of Propertius would seem to dictate. Thus the differences between the two poems, the distance traveled between the two languages, not only mark the intellectual positions of Propertius then and Pound now but are also a measure of the resilience, the durability, of the original, its power to virtually adapt itself to changed historical circumstances, as the poem acts upon itself through the translator's modulating responses.

More can be seen by going further. Pound completes the first small section (through l. 24 of the Latin) in essentially similar language. If anything, the enervated, decadent tone is nuanced by a more conspicuous hauteur and condescension:

> And besides, Lynceus,
>   you were drunk.
> Could you endure such promiscuity?
>   She was not known for fidelity;
> But to jab a knife in my vitals, to have passed on a swig of poison,
> Preferable my dear boy, my dear Lynceus,
> Comrade, comrade of my life, of my purse, of my person;
> But in one bed, one bed alone my dear Lynceus,
>   I deprecate your attendance;
> I would ask a like boon of Jove.

Patterns of repetition are drawn directly from the Latin:

> Comrade, comrade of my life . . .
> But in one bed, one bed alone . . .

from:

> te socium vitae, te corporis . . .
> lecto te solum, lecto te deprecor uno.

But whereas Propertius uses iteration as an expression of a certain (if conventionally rhetorical) intensity, Pound exaggerates the figure and makes repetition his very idiom, thereby destroying the usual effect of rhetorical artifice and indicating a cool, faintly bemused humor in its play of words:

> Preferable, my dear boy, my dear Lynceus . . .
> Comrade, comrade of my life, of my purse, of my person
> 　　　　　. . . my dear Lynceus.

Roughly the same tone predominates over the next fifteen lines that in the Latin review in some detail the inadequacy of Lynceus's background for his new amorous preoccupation.

> And you write of Achelous, who contended with Hercules
> You write of Adrastus' horses and the funeral rites of Achenor
> And you will not leave off imitating Aeschylus.
> 　　Though you make a hash of Antimachus,
> You think you are going to do Homer.
> 　　And still a girl scorns the gods,
> Of all these young women
> 　　not one has enquired the cause of the world,
> Nor the modus of the lunar eclipses
> 　　Nor whether there be any patch left of us
> After we cross the infernal ripples,
> 　　nor if the thunder fall from predestination;
> Nor anything else of importance.

Ellipsis is the most noticeable device here. A full twenty-two lines of the Latin are omitted, and Pound has left only the barest outlines of Propertius's train of thought. A Thebiad, Aeschylus, Homer, none of these lead to a lover's heart. Grand verse is an old habit to be broken. But while the Propertius didactically points out an appropriate poetic manner—

> tu satius memorem lusus imitere Philetan
> 　　et non inflati somnia Callimachi . . .
> incipe iam angusto versus includere torno
> 　　inque tuos ignes, dure poeta, veni . . .

—Pound's version carries no positive direction. All is phrased negatively, even the pleasing (in Propertius) literary and philosophical innocence of the "puella":

> Of all these young women
> 　　not one has enquired the cause of the world. . . .

Pound's voice, his intervening persona, has transmuted the bored care-lessness of the poem's earlier lines into a more coherent but utterly nihilistic poetic vision—"nor anything else of importance."

By now the force of the translation is established. We do not expect it to change. But Pound's language, as well as some of the emotional character of the poem, does alter in its twenty-eighth line: "Upon the Actian marshes Virgil is Phoebus' chief of police." Until now the poem's voice has presented itself as indifferent, careless of detail, conspicuously elliptical. Suddenly ellipsis all but disappears and "carelessness" modulates into flagrant "blunder" (the word of the *New Age* reviewer). This apparent shift of mode presents problems on several levels. Most obviously, whereas there was discernible compensation for the translation's "loss" in the first half of section 12 (a coherent interpretive intelligence is evident throughout), what precisely is gained in this second half by Pound's almost violently irregular "restitution" is less clear. Consider just a short section.

> tale facis carmen, docta testudine quale
>   Cynthius inpositis temperat articulis.
> non tamen haec ulli venient ingrata legenti,
>   sive in amore rudis sive peritus erit. . . .

> Like a trained and performing tortoise,
> I would make verse in your fashion, if she would command it,
> With her husband asking a remission of sentence,
>   And even this infamy would not attract numerous readers
> Were there an erudite or violent passion,
> For the nobleness of the populace brooks nothing below its
>   own altitude.
> One must have resonance, resonance and sonority . . .
>   like a goose.

We *can* easily perceive the general tenor of the adaptation. Enthusiastic praise for Vergil in the Latin is replaced by sarcastic defensiveness in the English. Vergil, as "Phoebus' chief of police" and apologist for Augustan empire, offers little of positive value to the Propertius that Pound sees—his distaste for even the Hellenistic Eclogues is evident. But beyond the obvious sarcasm and protest, deeper questions present themselves. Why does Pound depart so radically from the basic sense of the Latin? His often-employed ironic intonation and hyperbole could have accomplished the irreverence he wished to convey. What rationale governs the shift from Latin to English word? Can any system be isolated here, or is this just, as others have described it, free fantasy? If so, what is the point of such caprice in a translation that is at other times, on a word-for-word level, much more literal? To begin an answer, the logic of "like a trained and performing tortoise" for "docta testudine quale" is apparent. Ironic humor, its chief effect, derives from an obviously illiterate translation from one who, also obviously, knows better. Without both elements, adequate knowledge and intentional misprising, the line simply doesn't work. These are the dynamics of word play in any language; the tortoise shell lyre becomes a performing turtle, and we smile. But it is as if the pitch of absurdity sounded here is accelerated, and all trace of syntax and continuity in the Latin is lost. The relatively easy grammar of "tale facis carmen docta testudine quale / Cynthius inpositis temperat articulis" is shattered by Pound's treatment into discrete units, improbably interpreted. "Cynthius" (Cynthian Apollo) becomes by a humorous pun Cynthia's husband; "inpositis temperat articulis" has him tempering imposed articles, or a "sentence"; "haec . . . ingrata" is rendered "this infamy"; and homophonic word play can only account for the change from "sive in amore rudis, sive peritus erit" to "were there an erudite or violent passion." Through all this, the English—apart from its distortion of the Latin—never quite makes sense. We perceive an unmistakable tenor and "message" but find it difficult if not impossible to find coherence in individual lines. What precisely does "with her husband asking a remission of sentence" (and the following two lines) refer to or mean? The same question can be asked of any number of lines in this section:

> Head farmers do likewise, and lying weary among their oats
> They get praise from tolerant Hamadryads . . .
> Go on to Ascreus' prescription, the ancient, respected
>   Wordsworthian.
> And how ten sins can corrupt a maiden.

There are several ways of responding. One is to say simply that Pound has made any number of "major blunders" here and that his Latin is just not adequate to the task of making sense of Propertius. Or, merely a variation, that he has so misunderstood Propertius's mixture of irony and sincerity that he must distort him beyond all recognition whenever praise for Augustus or Vergil is expressed. Another approach is to assume creative word play, bilingual punning, pure and simple. Pound is having a bit of fun of the kind that should not, above all, be overanalyzed. Or perhaps (speaking of overanalysis) Pound is playing at some sort of deconstruction here, for after carefully establishing a translation that over the poem's first half plausibly and consistently delineates an interpretive vision of Propertius, Pound suddenly diverges technically and tonally and allows his interpretation, his translation, to collapse into itself. The tired and terse voice of the "superfluous man" has suddenly become that of an energetic and absurd, almost

Shakespearian, punster. The indeterminacy of text may be hinted at, the message that slips away, like the shade of Anchises, at the moment one most tries to clutch it. But that is not likely; Pound was not a man satisfied with indeterminacy, nor was he shy about stating in cold, concrete terms what sort of character his Propertius is. Similarly, the other views have had their hearings and have failed to convince entirely.

One must look elsewhere, particularly at any methodological consistencies between these radically dissimilar sections of the poem. We have noticed earlier Pound's tendency to translate in the manner of the persona he finds in Propertius. When he locates a fastidious note in the Latin (as in 3), he translates fastidiously, that is, closely, scrupulously. The hermeneutic motion is enacted and completed consistently. The translator-artist's "restitution" replaces, in kind, the loss incurred at the first interpretive encounter between poet and translator. The interpreted Propertius is, as it were, given the opportunity to recompose his poem. So too in 12: *Carmen* 2.34 plausibly suggests a Propertius who is distant, jaded, emotionally involved only on the level of rhetoric, careless of connection and structure. Pound's translation, as a product of that perceived sensibility, is equally careless of structure, detail, even "accuracy": if one considers all the implications of the word, it is "looser," just as Sullivan says.

But one must go beyond this fully to explain the apparent shift of strategy near the middle of this last poem. The Propertius of 2.34 is a love poet: from the beginning declaring his jealous passion, resuming his magisterial experience, and closing by including himself in the pantheon of amatory lyricists— Calvus, Catullus, Gallus, and the rest. In this theme of love Pound was not interested. But, as critics have noted, Pound saw an unacknowledged, perhaps more central, virtue in Propertius, his unmitigated loyalty to poetry itself and his desire to keep it free from the claims of the public and popular world.[23] Pound saw "love" in Propertius as essentially a metaphor for the poet's dedication to art. The translation thus begins in a deadened world. Love in the literal sense has lost its meaning; its language is indifferent, disconnected, empty. When Propertius comes to lay his claim to merit ("Cynthia quin etiam versu laudata Properti / hos inter si me ponere Fama volet"), therefore, Pound must establish grounds different from those that Propertius, at least explicitly, provides. And what he establishes in translating as he does is the elemental and intractable *poiesis* of the writer. He records and anatomizes the step from *datum* (in this case a text) to new poetic entity. He wants to demonstrate a process of intellect that *will be* precisely outrageous, surprising, spontaneous. Pound is not now concerned with "making sense" nor with finished product, but rather with the process of poetic rendering. And that secondary making is imaged in language that breaks free of readerly and translational expectations, a living art that turns impetuously to startling newness. In translation he has chosen a perfect vehicle to demonstrate the leap of mind that is his ultimate subject. It gives us beginning and end—and just an inkling (as it should be) of the mystery that comes between. *Ingenium*, not love, is Propertius's most enduring claim to our attention, and Pound would be right if he had merely pointed that out. He is miraculously right in recreating it.

Propertius, as a practitioner of the subjective love elegy, worked within a highly restrictive body of conventions; one measure of his accomplishment is the variation he was able to effect without changing the fundamental generic identity of the verse. A similar condition pertains to translation: the translator is limited by his text, but productive variety within those limits is often the mark of one's success—the revisionary translation is usually the most vital. Throughout, as we have seen, Pound revises as he feels a modern(-ist) Propertius might: the spirit of play and irony from "the road to Lanuvium" and anti-Augustan sarcasm, among many factors met and reckoned with in the progress of the translation, governing its changes. But Pound's redoubtable creative energies push translation to its conceptual limits. He clearly wanted it so. For in order to say what he does, finally, about Propertius, he must depend upon our ordinary expectations of translation as well as our surprise at the shifts and turns he works upon them. Translation that is more than translation; words that are more than words. So poetry.

> There is song in the parchment.

*   *   *

Section 12 closes on a subdued note as it stakes its serious claim to posterity. The theme in both the original and the translation is the undying value of love *transformed into song*, the surging of heart (for whatever reason) that makes for song.

> Varro sang of Jason's expedition
>   Varro, of his great passion Leucadia,
> There is song in the parchment; Catullus the highly indecorous,
> Of Lesbia, known above Helen;
> And in the dyed pages of Calvus,
>   Calvus mourning Quintilia,
> And but now Gallus had sung of Lycoris.
>   Fair, fairest Lycoris—
> The waters of Styx poured over the wound;
> And now Propertius of Cynthia, taking his stand among these.

It is an apt closing. It touches, too, on the dynamics and objectives of Pound's translation: the means of linking immediate experience to perpetual reexperience; the relation between inspiration and poem, and poem and translation; the themes of loyalty, dedication, and fidelity; and finally, declaration for the unorthodox, the exceptional, the few. Pound of Propertius "taking his stand among these." I have described here some of the ways Pound takes that stand. Only some. And, in focusing on the work as translation, I have overlooked much of both the poem and the poetry—a lapse excusable only by virtue of its urging the reader to reopen the old book and find it for himself again.

2

Memory's Tropes: Zukofsky's Catullus

P OUND was in the air, or his insistent and dogmatic voice in the ear of anyone who was anyone in the first half of our century. That is surely the kind of exaggeration promoted by the distorting attention of criticism. But in the smaller world of literary translation, it is arguable that he was just that prominent an influence. Specifically, it was the Pound of Propertius that translators heard, or poets heard and, hearing, realized that translation could be more than finger-exercise. It could be part of that tense Heraclitian stillness of "time past and time present" that Eliot sought. The classics were not, perhaps, (pulled from the casual discard of a later dark age) enjoying another renaissance but were, now more conspicuously remote, considered to be that *aition* of western literary consciousness which must somehow be brought into explicit relation with the present. That is not explanation enough, but, regardless of our imperfect anamneses and of our always inadequate understandings, we can at least be certain of sudden achieved richness in translation practice—after Pound's Propertius—of Latin and Greek material. It is a phenomenon that demands careful and critical exploration of the kind we have not done, in order that finally (*if* we are interested, after all) we may come to a few genuinely viable conclusions about the continuing life and pertinence of "the classical" in modern literature.

It is work that must be done piecemeal, since, for various reasons, we don't yet understand the pieces. Literary translations of even fine poets are still small beer to most critics and editors of the important literary histories. Moreover, some translations have been decidedly odd, threatening in their strangeness, and critics have walked around them. A few have bothered to stop and look these curious things over.[1]

> Zmyrna, my own Cinna, nine harvests passed making his hymn,
> Calm coped taste, nine harvesting, edited post wintering,
> Meanwhile there came out in one year king gander
> Hortensius you know
> [lacuna mss.]
> Zmyrna far as Satrachi pen it who's mid depth then the
> wonders,
> Zmyrna can a day or cycle bear all you intend.

But Volusius' *Annals,* Padua more adventurous out fishing
   Mackeral, 'll skim rip its pages wrapping a catch.
Purvey me my intimate's core, dear monument's all that
                                    there is,
   let the populace (tumid or gaudy) eat Antimacho.

Zmyrna mei Cinna, nonam post denique messem
     quam coeptast nonamque edita post heimem,
milia cum interea quingenta Hortensius uno
. . . .
Zmyrna cavas Satrachi penitus mittetur ad undas,
   Zmyrnam cana diu saecula pervolvent.
at Volusi annales Paduam morientur ad ipsam
   et laxas scombris saepe dabunt tunicas.

                                            (95)

"This translation of Catullus follows the sound, rhythm, and syntax of his Latin—tries, as is said, to breathe the literal meaning with him." That, aside from a scholarly note on the arrangement of Catullus's poems, is the entirety of Louis and Celia Zukofsky's preface to their complete Catullus (1969). The project is an odd one. Louis Zukofsky, the American poet who coined the tag "objectivism" and with Bunting and Williams developed ideas given first impulse by Pound's imagism, and who matured to become one of the more significant voices in American poetry, was not a frequent translator of classical literature. Apart from his versions of Catullus, his only other extant classical translation is a version of the *Rudens* imbedded in his long sequence of poems, "A." The single sentence of the preface to the Catullus does little to clarify the poet's motivation and artistic objectives, and intital reactions to the project may be negative. On first glance the reader will notice the following: of the three components of Catullus's Latin itemized by the translators, the first (sound) seems to govern (though usually very loosely) English word choice, the second (rhythm) is seldom observed with accuracy, and the third (syntax) is a manifest impossibility. We have, in short, what is normally called a homophonic translation—the sort of thing that is interesting, usually, for a poem or two but soon loses its appeal. Indeed, this translation has not been well received. Burton Raffel (1969, 440):

> To whom is this "translation" of Catullus . . . of any use? The Latinist can read Catullus in Latin; he does not need, nor presumably is he interested to read, that [from 26] 'o ventrum horribilem atque pestilentem' can be aped (but not translated, no) as 'o vent them horrible, I'm out quite, pestilent mm.' The non-Latinist wants to know, as well as he can, what Catullus said and how he said it. Can he get anything—*anything*?—from this?

Alan Brownjohn: "[T]he Zukofskys have painstakingly copied the sound of the Latin, wrenching it into a crazy approximation of modern English. . . .

It all reads like hopeful stabs at unseen translation when one hasn't done the homework of the night before: knotted, clumsy, turgid, and ultimately silly. . . ." (1969, 151). And Conquest, who, as with Pound and his sympathizers, relishes the role of literary curmudgeon: "The Hun is at play—worse still, *at work*—among the ruins" (1970, 56).[2]

So far, bare reactions. Kelly, while still disapproving (he "converts Catullus to Gertrude Stein"), goes a step further by placing the translation in a framework of ideas—that of "symbolist" translation (a term derived from Buhler's "three functions of language"). This, in turn, locates it in a context of traditional notions drawn most prominently of late from Benjamin:

> [I]t is [an approach] indifferent to anything beyond the units of the text, including an intended reader. Benjamin begins with a blunt denial that translation is meant for a reader, and there is a "content" that can be communicated without damage to the integrity of the task. Thus at the outset he restricts his object to literary translation and to translation in the Symbolist sense of commuting word to word. . . . Underneath a translation, one must see the movements of the original. In this way, through the clash between the surface structures of the two languages, one will find what they have in common, which is the pure language, the *logos* (Kelly 1979, 54–55).

Certainly, Zukofsky's "to breathe the literal meaning with [Catullus]" would seem to confirm this intent. But that places it in spirit next to the infamous practice of Browning in his *Agamemnon*, who strove "to be literal at every cost save that of absolute violence to our language." A sense of what Browning meant by "absolute violence" may be inferred from what he considers acceptable:

> The gods I ask deliverance from these labors,
> Watch of a year's length whereby, slumbering through it
> On the Atreidai's roof on elbow,—dog like—
> I know of nightly star-groups the assemblage,
> And those that bring to men winter and summer,
> Bright dynasts, as they pride them in the aether
> —stars, when they wither, and the uprisings of them.

The Aeschylus:

> θεοὺς μὲν αἰτῶ τῶνδ' ἀπαλλαγὴν πόνων,
> φρουρᾶς ἐτείας μῆκος, ἣν κοιμώμενος
> στέγαις 'Ατρειδῶν ἄγκαθεν, κυνὸς δίκην,
> ἄστρων κάτοιδα νυκτέρων ὁμήγυριν,
> καὶ τοὺς φέροντας χεῖμα καὶ θέρος βροτοῖς
> λαμπροὺς δυνάστας, ἐμπρέποντας αἰθέρι
> ἀστέρας, ὅταν φθίνωσιν ἀντολαῖς τε τῶν.

As to the Zukofsky, most readers have responded harshly to this version—not least (as quoted above) Pound: "What Browning had not got into his sometimes excellent top knot was the patent, or what should be the patent fact, that inversions of sentence order in English are not, simply and utterly *are not* any sort of equivalent for inversions and perturbations of order in a language inflected as Greek and Latin are inflected" ("Translators," 148). Pound's dogmatism is persuasive and is on the literal level perfectly just: but there is a sense in which it is misleading. Clearly, a Pindaric or Horatian ode differs in its independence from the more common word orders found in classical comedy, satire, and most prose. The reason is simple: the old rhetorical devices of hyperbaton and anastrophe are traditional markers of formal, artificial, usually "elevated" verse. In such a situation, a "piecing-together" is required, even by native speakers, although their power of holding verbal elements in suspension until they are syntactically resolved is naturally more developed and deeply ingrained than ours. But still, an effort, a conscious shift to another frequency. Is this anything more than what Browning asks of his readers? Certainly, after a little sorting through of the syntax the sense is clear enough. It is apparent, also, that while the Greek word order is a dominant force in Browning's version, it is not followed absolutely, so that rather than attempting an "equivalence" as Pound would have it, Browning seems to want to offer in his English an analogical vestige of the Greek. The "clash between the surface structures of the two languages" quite consciously takes precedence over idiomatic fluency. The "direction" of translation, as Arrowsmith somewhere has it, changes. The reader is in some sense "translated back" to the original rather than text translated forward into a contemporary frame. Such a method is usually, and correctly, indicted for its inability to capture "tone"; but, as all methodologies fail in some respect, it is not per se an execrable idea.

With Zukofsky,[3] phonetics operate in place of Browning's word order. But, like Browning, he is juxtaposing surface structures of languages and wrenching English out of its conventional idiom. But with what differences? The hostile reception of Zukofsky's "phonemic"[4] method surely sets it apart even from the company of Hölderlin and Browning. Four general objections have been made in André Lefèvre's detailed critique (1975, 20–26): (1) Phonemic translation does not accurately reflect the sound of the Latin but merely approximates it in filtering it "through the phonemic grid of the target language" (1975, 20). Thus, "calm coped taste, Nine harvesting, edited post wintering" only partially approximates "quam coeptast nonamque edita post hiemem." (2) It often depends on verbal "padding"—using too many English words to capture the syllable count of the Latin. So, "meanwhile there came out in one year" for "milia cum interea." (3) The method, in its search for aural similarity, may utilize (by necessity?) the odd or archaic word. So, "coped" in the lines quoted above meaning "vested" or "clothed." (4) Part and parcel of this phonemic translation is the attempt to pull the English words out of normal order. This requires the reader to engage in the "childish game" (as Lefèvre calls it) of construing the English. So, "*Zmyrna* far as Satrachi pen it who's mid-depth there the wonders" must be "sorted through" to find in it a rough paraphrase of the Latin: "*Zmyrna cavas Satrachi penitus mittetur ad undas.*" The inconsistencies in sense are obvious, and practically none of the lines in poem 95 are rendered without some quite plain revision of literal meaning. Worse still, the divergence is so radical that restitution of sense sometimes simply fails when one depends upon the English alone: "All too often the much sought equilibrium between dominance of sound and undercurrent of meaning is shattered. What remains are a few blessed oases of plain sense, devoid of successful sound-imitation, between vast bewildering stretches of moderately successful sound-imitation either altogether void of immediate sense or running contrary to the sense of the source text" (Lefèvre 1975, 26).

Given the expectations of the critics mentioned above, none of these objections is in fact answerable. But Zukofsky's poem 95 is dedicated to Ezra Pound, the man who has taught us to revise our expectations. Perhaps answers may be found, then, in another look, one illuminated by the efforts of Pound half a century earlier. Of course, homophonic word play is found everywhere in the *Homage* to Propertius (though obviously that is not the fundamental principle of translation there), but the earlier *Seafarer* gives us Pound's most famous exercise in the method: "reckon" for *wrecan* (to make, compose), "stern" for *stearn* (a tern), "moaneth" for *monath* (makes mindful of, urges) and the rest.[5] So,

> Waneth the watch, but the world holdeth.
> Tomb hideth trouble. The blade is layed low.
> Earthly glory ageth and seareth.

For:

> wuniath the wacran   and thas woruld healdath,
> brucath thurh bisgo.   Blaed is gehnaeged;
> eorthan indryhto   ealdath and searath.
>   (87–89)

While scholars aplenty have panned the result, Michael Alexander, who has done his share of Anglo-Saxon translating, remarks,

> The closeness to the sound and word order of the original forces the reader's tongue to twist through the articulation of the original, right down to the gristly sounds themselves. He is not rendering the sense of the Anglo-Saxon into standard literary English, but rather making the minimum modernization of the Old English to accommodate it to modern understanding; that is why his syntax is so tortuous elsewhere. He breaks the mold, gets beneath the reader's guard, by his dislocation

of conventional responses; one is forced to consider the Old English not as notation but as actual speech, so refractory are its patterns. The pastness, the uncompromising difference of the past, appears; and yet what it says is intelligible, dynamic, even compelling. (1979, 74)

Pound breaks the mold (later, the pentameter). And it is clear that, for all its greater contempt for ordinary sense, Zukofsky's Catullus is an echo of this impulse.[6]

Another parallel. An element that must subliminally irk the critics is the scholarly layout of Zukofsky's book: oversized and entitled pretentiously, *Catullus (Gai Valeri Catulli Veronensis Liber)*. Facing pages contain text and translation. The translator's preface, already quoted in part, concludes with this standard information put maybe a shade too technically: "The skip from 17 to 20 in the sequence of the poems is traditional, after the earliest codices, Codex Oxoniensis (late 14C.) and Codex Sangermanensis or Parisiensis (c. 1375). Modern scholars usually include Carmen 18 (fragment 2 in our book) with the fragmenta of the canon, but omit carmina 19 and 20 as spurious." This all seems a little too enthusiastically "Latin" (there's even a bit of hypercorrection in the "Parisiensis" for the more usual "Parisinus"). We wonder why. We want to read Zukofsky's poetry, not his scholarship. But a help, again, is Pound, who was there first. His *Seafarer* appends this "Philological Note":

> The text of this poem is rather confused. I have rejected half of line 76 [and on in this vein]. . . . There are many conjectures as to how the text came into its present form. It seems most likely that a fragment of the original poem, clear through about the first thirty lines, and thereafter increasingly illegible, fell into the hands of a monk with literary ambitions who filled in the gaps with his own guesses and "improvements". . . .(Ruthven 1969, 214)

This is what Pound called " 'New Method' in Literary Scholarship" and what skeptics might describe as the pot talking down to the kettle. But the point is not to quibble. Nor to gainsay New Methods in Literary Scholarship in Pound or Zukofsky, but to see what, poetically, they may have been pointing to.

The tone and "rhetoric" of scholarship conveys several notions among which knowledge and authority are only the most obvious (and are naturally those to which critics are most sensitive when they see them manifested in poets). But it conveys, too, a sense of care, of respect for the (even archaic) poetic voice, a naturally retrospective as well as prospective sensitivity. Indubitably secondary in nature, scholarship approaches its text with diffidence. It is a method of inquiry, an interrogative mode. So may be translation. The spirit represented by Zukofsky's scholarly format and language is precisely this. Of course, rather than establishing another definitive text of Catullus, he is setting upon a serious and systematic exploration of the Latin text using the sophisticated equipment he has to hand, his language, his art. This is why Guy Davenport's sympathetic reception of the work perhaps misses the mark just a bit: "[I]ts native enterprise is to *play*. . . . The immediate sense must be that of *ludens*—the play of thought over a subject. This sense must not be detached from that of *playing* music. Neither discursive, nor incantatory, nor molendinary, Zukofsky's poetry is a playing of the intellect over a choice inventory of observations and predilections" (1970, 130). That would do nicely for a goodly number of modern poets, among them Stevens and Auden, but misses the essential point of Zukofsky's consideration, interrogation, of text, which in turn is patterned upon Pound's "New Method" that sought to realize the primitive base of the *Seafarer*'s Anglo-Saxon, the "English National Chemical" (Alexander 1979, 76). In that translation, Pound claimed to be "as nearly literal, I think, as any translation can be"; in his preface, Zukofsky announced an intention "to breathe the 'literal' meaning with [Catullus]." Both were quite serious and were up to considerably more than play. It will justify spending a few moments attempting to discover how so apparently nonliteral a rendering as Zukofsky's can be what he says it is and can have, as Pound was to claim for his Propertius, scholarly value.

XI

Furi et Aureli, comites Catulli,
sive in extremos penetrabit Indos,
litus ut longe resonante Eoa
    tunditur unda,
sive in Hyrcanos Arabasve molles,
seu Sagas sagittiferosque Parthos,
sive quae septemgeminus colorat
    aequora Nilus,
sive transaltas gradietur Alpes,
Caesaris visens monimenta magni,
Gallicum Rhenum, horribilesque ulti-
    mosque Britannos,
omnia haec, quaecumque feret voluntas
caelitum, temptare simul parati,
pauca nuntiate meae puellae
    non bona dicta.
cum suis vivat valeatque moechis,
quos simul complexa tenet trecentos,
nullum amans vere, sed identidem omnium
    ilia rumpens:
nec meum respectet, ut ante, amorem,
qui illius culpa cecidit velut prati

ultima flos, praeter eunte postquam
    tactus aratrost.

11

Furius, Aurelius: comities—Catullus
If he penetrate most remote India,
lit as with the long resonant coast East's wave
    thundering under—
if in Hyrcania, mull of Arabia,
say the Sacae, arrow ferocious Parthians,
why even the seven gamming mouth, colored
    ichor of Nilus—
even that Transalpine graded tour magni-
fying visions of our Caesar's monuments,
Gallic Rhine, and the horrible ultimate
    mask of the Britons—
on hand, men, come whatever gods ferret and
want of us, you who're always prompt to feel with
me, take a little note now to my darling,
    no kind word dictates.
May she live, and avail herself, in the moist
clasp of one concourse of three hundred lechers,
loving no man's ever, and doomed to drain all
    men who must rupture:
no, let her not look back at me as she used to,
at her love whose fault was to die as at some
meadow's rim, the blossom under the passing
    cut of the share's thrust.

The Latin is, it is commonly presumed, Catullus's farewell to Lesbia, the bitter closure to a literary affair that began with the famous overture in *Carmen* LI,[7] his translation of Sappho. Zukofsky's rendering is one of the most conventional of his collection. The sound of words still guides their choice when convenient, but he is not bound strictly to the homophonic rule. What is more, the sense is quite clear, and in its mimicry (to the eye at least) of Catullus's Sapphics we are reminded very much of Pound's intention in the *Seafarer* and sections of the *Homage*. Still, it is not entirely a conventional bit of work.

"Comities" translates "comites." Catullus is being ironic in addressing Furius and Aurelius as "companions" but delicately so. His extended list of (hypothetical) shared adventures and journeys—evidence of their solidarity—has been seen by Horace and others as positive evidence of good fellowship (although Catullus has little good to say of this pair in other of his poems). Yet the radical shift in tone at line 17 has led many readers to sense exaggerated ceremony, an artificial inflation of language, in this first long protasis. So "comities," a word related to "comes" ("companion") but less personal, more formal in implication—"courtesies," "civilities"—takes a position. The old tag, "false friend," captures both the essential dissonance of the two words and the semantic implication of the change. The first line, then, reads with a touch of irony. But rather than rush headlong into a radically ironical interpretation, the next few lines withdraw into what is for the most part the ordinary sense of the Latin. "Mull of Arabia," though dictated by considerations of sound, does not wrench the poem into any strange new light and captures nicely in its lexical rarity just the sense of exotic effeminacy that the Latin hints at. So, too, the odd but plausible "seven gamming mouth" and the *almost* inert nuancing of "sagittiferos" to "arrow ferocious." Even the "horrible ultimate / masks of the Britons" embodies a certain propriety of tone. But "that Transalpine graded tour magni-/ fying visions of our Caesar's monuments" again becomes adventurous in extending rather than representing the gentle irony of the Latin. The Poundian tone in "graded tour" demeans Caesar directly and sends the whole phrase into sarcasm. There is little genuine nostalgia, then, for *this* shared experience.

Through the first fifteen lines, then, Zukofsky has posited an interpretation that moves toward a more explicit irony, but hesitantly, as if testing whether the Latin will bear the heavier burden of his more strongly colored English. The translation moves in and out of the Latin, now essaying a strong word, now falling back into more literal transfers to contain the revisionary energies within the general semantic frame of the Latin. It is almost as if the two voices, one Zukofsky, one Catullus, in designed alternation (deriving from Pound's experiments with Propertius) come to prominence in the translation: so, a sense of dialogue.[8] An immediate effect is that when we come to the bitter penultimate stanza, we are better prepared for it than we are in the Latin.

> May she live, and avail herself, in the moist
> clasp of one concourse of three hundred lechers,
> loving no man's ever, and doomed to drain all
>   men who must rupture.

The tone of the language, too, is more consistent, preserving the same off-key formality that governed the first four stanzas. A hint of the absurd. We lose, however, the shock of the sudden pitch into vitriol, of the cutting sarcasm that is, precisely, not absurd but excruciatingly real. Still, Zukofsky's is not a misdirected effort—his view suggesting only a slightly more distanced and cooler frame of mind that is perhaps itself a comment on the nature of a translation's relation to its model.

The method of Catullus's poem, we recall, is to lead on his interlocutors, Furius and Aurelius, with flattering graciousness, just as he feels himself to have been led on by Lesbia's deceit. Until the penultimate stanza, where, with a sharp twist of the knife, Catullus recreates the sense of betrayal. There, Furius and Aurelius, in the fictional frame of the poem, would realize that not friendship but a certain aptness of character suits them for this ugly mission (compare their treatment in *Carmina* XVI, XXI, XXIII, XXIV, XXVI). Zukofsky the translator knows all this. Yet translation is, like scholarship, secondary, and its business (for Zukofsky, Pound, and many others) is not to mimic but to somehow illuminate by embodying both the ancient and modern perspectives, to somehow capture the distance between. Hence, this translation seeks not to imitate the sudden turn or the "naïve" voice of the first few stanzas but, from its position of experience and distance, to make the latent signals of irony in the Latin more explicit—to sketch out the voice *behind* the Catullan persona.

The test of it all is the relative coherence of each version with respect to the poem's famous final stanza containing Catullus's most compelling image (itself borrowed from Sappho). Here Zukofsky has almost completely abandoned the homophonic method. The evocative power of the Latin *sense* is allowed full stage. In both languages the effect of the stanza is impressive. Catullus provides here just reason for his outburst of bile; Zukofsky gives equally sufficient reason for his nudges toward a more explicitly ironical diction.

> nec, meum respectet, ut ante, amorem,
> qui illius culpa cecidit velut prati
> ultimi flos, praetereunte postquam
>   tactus aratrost.
>
> no, let her not look at me as she used to,
> at her love whose fault was to die as at some
> meadow's rim, the blossom under the passing
>   cut of the share's thrust.

The only hint of word-rhyme here is "share's thrust" for "aratrost." In a stanza given over almost entirely to the sense of Catullus's Latin, Zukofsky closes, confidently, with a bold homophone having no semantic parallel in the original. Is the poet indicating that aural resonance alone can offer sufficient connection between words, languages? "Aratrost": the long "o" and the effort of the trilled "r" following the dental stop overwhelm the passivity of "tactus . . . est." "Thrust" is somehow just right, even if it compounds the simple innocence of the image with sexual innuendo from the previous stanza. But, of course, the hint was already there—the trope was old long before Shakespeare's jokes about plowing. The words, semantically unrelated ("thrust" not even being latinate), take on a kind of sympathetic harmony. The English enacts a reconnaissance in the expressive field of the Latin, takes on some of the Latin character (its sound), and returns to its English frame richer and more complex for the journey. The format of the translation tells us this much; it is facing-page. We are intended to see the two poems in juxtaposed interaction, intended to note not merely that "comites" and "comities," say, loosely rhyme, but the way in which the two words signify—collaboratively. The central and informing idea of Zukofsky's homophonic method is that it provides a system of relation which is precisely not ordinary semantic bartering but one that allows an exploring, an enrichment, a building of word upon word. Aural affinity is, then, nothing more than a key to a more complex poetic purpose, a compounding and deepening of meaning.

We see it in 51, in Catullus the poem of initial overture to Lesbia and thus the analogue to XI (both, of course, are written in Sapphics). Here the homophonic methodology is much more extremely presented.

> Ille mi par esse deo videtur,
> ille, si fas est, superare divos,
> qui sedens adversus identidem te
>   spectat et audit
> dulce ridentem, misero quod omnis
> eripit sensus mihi: nam simul te,
> Lesbia, aspexi, nihil est super mi
>   [vocis in ore]
> lingua sed torpet, tenuis sub artus
> flamma demanat, sonitu suopte
> tintinant aures, gemina teguntur
>   lumina nocte.

> He'll hie me, par *is* he? the God divide her,
> he'll hie, see fastest, superior deity,
> quiz—sitting adverse identity—mate, in-
>   spect it and audit—
> you'll care ridden then, misery hold omens,
> air rip the sense from me; now you smile to
> me—Lesbia's aspect—no life is to spare me
>   [voice hoarse in throat]
> linked tongue set torpid, tenuous support a-
> flame a day mown down, sound tone sopped up in its
> tinkling, in ears hearing, twin eyes tug under
>   luminous—a night.

A translation that, for all its wonderful Hopkinsian noise,[9] most would find nonsensical. A flip, misguided extrapolation from the Latin—precisely, sound and fury signifying nothing. Even those liking the poem will find their ingenuity strained to discover a reason in this madness. The rivalry theme of the original is there, of course, and appropriately in the first stanza. The archaic "hie" is apt enough too, hurrying, the race, competition; even the radical sense of "pant" is not inapposite. But "the God divide her" presents problems. In what sense "divide"? What God? And how does one read line 3 for denoted sense? And who, exactly, is the "you" of lines 5 and 6? We are not allowed definitive answers to these questions, but the lines do come clearer if one presumes the Latin, i.e., if the Latin poem, sound and sense, becomes a necessary part of the interpretive context of the English.[10]

The original is familiar enough to make discussion at this point a bit easier. Catullus is translating the famous *Phainetai moi* (Fragment 31) of Sappho and for the first few stanzas making subtle changes in the poem's tone and character, which in sum tend to make the poem less immediate, a bit more "literary." Catullus compares his rival to a god since he has Lesbia's attention. Zukofsky's "God" must then be the rival himself who "divides her" from the poem's speaker. And this marks another shift; Catullus has not "had" Lesbia yet—the poem portrays their initial meeting. But the tone of the translation's first line (and, as we'll see, of the whole poem) speaks as if of an intruder into an established romance. Thus, the indignation of the emphasized "par *is* he?" the disdainful "quiz— . . .—mate," the threat of "you'll care ridden then," the hint of intimate experience in "Lesbia's aspect." In short, we find Zukofsky working changes—systematic and coherent changes—that presume a knowledge of Catullus LI, and, further, of the whole course of the affair seen through the Lesbia poems. There is especially in this translation a great deal of *Carmen* XI, the resentment, the disquiet: "misery hold omens." The key of the Latin's *participation* in this translation seems to solve much of its difficulty. The "you" is at least on one obvious level the rival, not Lesbia who is the addressee of the original; hence the not-so-veiled threat ("you'll care ridden then") to one less experienced. But in the following line, "you" is again Lesbia: "now you smile to me." This shifting of focus leads to a deeper complexity. "Sitting adverse identity." The initial "you," the rival, is in some sense "Catullus" himself. "You'll care ridden then" looks forward to the Catullus of *Carmen* XI or of any number of poems in the Lesbia sequence. But particularly XI—the phrase effectively links the two poems, one on each end of the central Catullan experience. Poems, then, "inspect it and audit"—especially Zukofsky's in that last word.

However one reads Zukofsky's success in this, his process is not facile or glib. It does less than "translate" in the most conventional sense (one must be able to use the Latin at least a little) and more than poetically gloss. In impetus, his method derives most anciently from Cicero, but most immediately from Pound who began to forge new connections between poem and translation, to break down the simple model of sense for sense. Zukofsky has carried the thing further, in ways Pound would not. And yet his poem 51 *is* a translation in that its sense and being depend upon its relation to an original. Each bit of the translation—in the reading—looks back to the Latin for orientation, for the reason of its changes. The homophonic system, if we can avoid thinking it merely an arbitrary lark, tells us this. The Latin sounds to us in the English, but changed, Americanized. The sense of the Latin has to be there as well—so the scholarly tone of the preface intimates—then, too, is changed, developed along lines of novel or perhaps "belated" poetic intent. The translator's method is thus recursive, and the sense of the new poem is similarly recursive—"sitting adverse identity"—end to beginning, beginning to end, hope to despair and back. And, finally, the physical manifestation of the emotion that governs all this poetic energy in Catullus:

> linked tongue set torpid, tenuous support a-
> flame all day mown down, sound tone supped up in its
> tinkling, in ears humming, twin eyes tug under
>   luminous—a night.

Sappho had made this a painfully precise itemization of the physiology of jealous emotion: the burning, awful experience. Catullus made it more stylized, less detailed, artful in its rhymes, alliterations, and rhetoric. Zukofsky, presuming this progress, has made here a brilliant synthesis of the personal and the abstract. Beginning with a memory of the Latin meaning, the English verse loosely echoes that sense even while it audaciously pursues its own course. Sappho, overcome by jealous emotion, describes her tongue as "broken" (*glossa eage*); Catullus, in translating, merely has it paralyzed ("lingua sed torpet"); Zukofsky suggests both ("linked tongue set torpid")— but not merely to synthesize. A "linked tongue" is one of two "chained" (or one broken to two); the theme of doubleness and antithesis is reiterated: day and night, light and darkness, "twin eyes." And, again, the two poems: in one that announces love's beginning, we find the dominant image, piercingly sad, of the second (XI) announcing love's end—"mown down." The last line of Zukofsky 51 is a perfectly resolving conclusion: "luminous—a night."

And so, what is normally the fourth and final stanza of LI is translated separately (called by Zukofsky "51a" following some texts, although most, with reservations, include it in the body of LI).[11] But whereas others see this Sapphic as altogether alien in intent from the three preceding stanzas, Zukofsky makes it a summary. This is an astute bit of interpreting, since the suggestion that this is the intended function of the problematic fourth stanza is present in the Latin—though often overlooked. Catullus, in translating this Sappho for a new and lovely acquaintance, has made an overture. Then, in the hyperbolic manner of the lover, he derides the folly of his hopes:

> otium, Catulle, tibi molestum est:
> otio exsultas nimiumque gestis:

> otium et reges prius et beatas
>   perdidit urbes.

But Catullus's manner is playful; he is only mildly chagrined by the possibility of failure. Zukofsky, on the other hand, is full of dark premonition:

> O the time, Catullus, to be molests you:
> O tedious exults in you, in your quaint jests.
> O the time it rages pre-us, to be at us,
>   peers who died, or orbs.

The lines speak for themselves. It is enough to note again the themes of premonition, duality, antithesis, love and loss. The "time to be" is of course also the poem to be, *Carmen* XI, and the richness of temporal play in the two poems is intimated in the third line—"O the time it rages pre-us, to be at us." "Peers" of the fourth line recalls "par" of the first line of 51, the radical sense of both words being simply "equal" or a "pair." "Peers who died" remembers "a-flame a day mown down," and "orbs," "twin eyes tug under luminous—a night." Through all this the Latin is there, not hovering vaguely under the play of Zukofsky's words but vividly and essentially contributing, completing the English sense. Zukofsky, always, creates in his translation, carries given meaning further than one expects, further than most approve of. But the fact that all this is not merely a capricious and undisciplined fantasia is demonstrated in the way the English persistently turns us back to the Latin. There it is on the facing page, as alive and crucial to the business of poetic making (or making sense) as ever it was. Nor will it quite do to say that the Catullus is "alive and crucial" only for Latinists, unless one means by that anyone with curiosity enough to struggle a little between text and trot. And whereas ponies will feebly stand in for their original, this translation insists on pulling us back in thought and time to the truth of the poem. Zukofsky's work enacts the process of poetic memory and demands that we undergo that same process. In so doing, it nudges the art of translation beyond another frontier. There is no question of this translation's "standing alone"; Zukofsky might aver that no poem, ever, "stands alone" and certainly not a translation. The doubleness that governs the images of 51 stands here too as an emblem of essential interdependence, poem and translation.

And elsewhere. Even the long poems at the center of the Catullan corpus—ambitious reads in either the Latin or Zukofsky's rendering—redeem the significant time spent in sorting through the collaboration of languages. With wit:

> cum lecti iuvenes, Argivae robora pubis
>
> came elect young ones ace, Argive eye robe awry pubes.

Or perceptive development:

> sicine discedens neglecto numine divum
> immemor a, devota domum periuria portas?

> See can you discard hence neglect our numina devious
> in memory, devoted homing—perjuries are portals?

So Ariadne, in this last, reproaches the cad (Theseus) who abandoned her. There is surprising achievement, too, in the epigrams. There may be no richer presentation of the theme of betrayed friendship than this from 73:

> quam modo qui me unum atque unicum amicum habuit

> qualm mode o quick my one—who that quick knew the one me—
>   gone become habit.

∗   ∗   ∗

O the time it rages. . . .

Augustine, as everyone knows, in addressing the huge, intractable issue of time and its perception in the eleventh book of his *Confessions*, found the key to its comprehension in memory. A psalm, remembered before it is once again recited, located for him a sense of past, present, and future—and a measure for all of them. Eliot, recalling Augustine and Heraclitus and Krishna, works his turns on the old issue in his *Four Quartets:*

> That the future is a faded song, a Royal Rose
>   or a lavender spray
> Of wistful regret for those who are not yet here to regret,
> Pressed between yellow leaves of a book that has never
>   been opened.
>   ("The Dry Salvages")

Zukofsky is less explicit, but he knows that translation, at least in part, is a grand experiment with time. One makes it new; brings a reader back or a text forward; classics in dead languages are given, we are told, "new life." And he knows, as did Augustine, that memory is the key to that experiment, that translation invokes, makes manifest in its workings, our poetic memories, embodies them.

3

"And Wit Its Soul": Modern Martials

In lapidary totals go the water-woken syllables.
—L. Durrell

WE know that translation can sometimes embody rhapsody. It can also incite an almost rhapsodic enthusiasm in its commentators, as in Steiner occasionally *(After Babel)* or Frederick Will thinking of Steiner thinking of translation:

> Translating is a special kind of navigating inside the unposted ocean of consciousness. The translator exists par excellence as the mind discovering what is immersed in a boundariless *langue*. To translate, even more than to create, is to look around your language, to experience it as a constantly self-proposing collection of possibilities, a collection seemingly inexhaustible, and most clearly so when an effort is made to exhaust it. . . . (1975, 973)

Or Robert Bagg on the abyss between Homer's time and ours purposefully manifested in Robert Fitzgerald's rendering:

> At the moment we experience Odysseus and Penelope weeping at last in each other's arms, we find entering that feeling the unimaginable sensation of washing ashore at the glad land, out of range of a god's hatred, and rolling in upon our completed knowledge of the long, painful way home across the seas, flowing through the embrace and carrying us backward in thought. (1969, 65)

"Backward in thought" suggests a kind of miracle, the fantasy of a time machine whose magical mechanics are scholarship and poetry. Homer's world here or our eyes there. Zukofsky's poetics of memory come writ large in some views; more than memory, a reexperiencing, or the sharp if evanescent frisson of touching something remarkably other.

But these are not universal views. Many, even those compulsively interested, are decidedly less transported by the subject—the redoubtable B.L. Gildersleeve, for instance:

> Translation and no end! If the malevolent reader will scan the list of *Books Received* [in the *American Journal of Philology*], he may behold

70

to the satisfaction of his wicked heart how many versions there are to challenge criticism, how many rival renderings to demand comparison. And there is no sharper knife wherewith to pry the classical oyster out of his shell than the familiar questions one encounters in literary and semi-literary circles: "What to you think of Mr. Somebody's translation?" (1975, 950)

And this crotchety offhandedness from a man who counts himself "no enemy of translation" and who can cite approvingly Wilamowitz's term, "metempsychosis," for the art, justly, creatively accomplished. The obvious point is that translation presents various faces to various readers and translators. Not always the complicated and mysterious act of secondary *poiesis* of relatively recent critical rumination, it has often been and continues to be for many a limited exercise, a yeoman's craft, always restricted in some sense by the ineluctable fact of another poet's *datum*—"restricted" if one wants to see it that way, and many do. The translator travels pillion behind his "genuinely creating" poet—however much he may wish to push him off and take the horse another way.

This sense of cool reservation derives not so much from Roger Bacon or Quine (in their different ways) telling us of the insuperable limitations of translation, nor is it a matter only of individuals' differing minds. Rather it has to do with literary "climate," of what translation means to an age. And that is a large issue, involving not only the nature of the translation itself but the kinds of things chosen for new rendering, how that is managed, and what the dominant tenor of the time's original poetry is. Still we know why Livius Andronicus, say, translated Homer; Terence, Menander; Cicero, his philosophers; Catullus, his Sappho and Callimachus; and the sheer multiplicity of intent and effect represented by these important translators prompts us to consider our own period a little more carefully, to see, in verse and translation, beyond the strong strokes of Poundian experiment and the pyrotechnics of modernism.

* * *

Apposite may be T.S. Eliot's reaction to a decidedly non-modernist and not very popular genre. He didn't much like it; though he felt that it constituted a useful "rebellion against the romantic tradition which insists that a poet should be continuously inspired." He continued, "If we only knew 'perfect' poetry we should know very little about poetry."[1] Faint praise, that, but Ezra Pound, in reference to whom Eliot was writing, did like it for a time at least and employed it conspicuously in his 1915 *Lustra*. Pound felt that this, for its kind, was perfect enough:

> Phyllidula is scrawny but amorous,
> Thus have the gods awarded her
> That in pleasures she receives more than she can give:

If she does not count this blessed
Let her change her religion.

The lowly epigram. Pound once thought to claim "Phyllidula" as a translation from "Antipater of Cos," then, thinking better of it, let it stand as an independent poem. Even lacking an original, however, he has the thing right. Plain language, brevity, a theme from ordinary experience, an element of coarseness, a simple yet surprising ironic "turn"—all put into place and relation by a perceptive and acute intellect. These are at least some of the stock elements we have come to associate with the genre, and they combine pleasingly here. But, ironically, the conventional harmony of this poem is a kind of trap and one that Pound himself for the most part avoided. That trap is the facile categorization of the genre and a consequent delimitation of its poetic range and flexibility.

The epigram is a marvelously mutable thing. It began in Greece sometime before our first evidences from the seventh century and was then simply what it was called, a "writing-upon" or inscription for tombstones and the like, usually in elegiac meter. But from this simplest of beginnings its applications ramified. Asclepiades and Meleager made it a vehicle for subjective reflection; others used it for more extroverted and literary purposes. Pastoral elements occurred not infrequently. By the third century, its range of possible themes and styles was almost intractably broad.[2] The next dramatic revision of the genre therefore served to focus it: Lucilius (the Neronian, not the earlier satirist) introduced conspicuous use of hyperbole, humor, and ironic point—devices that were taken up by Martial and have come to dominate the popular sense of the epigram. In so dominating, these devices (much later) modulated the genre into moribund formulae, overpainting much of its rich subtlety with the broader strokes of simple satire and blunt irony.

Pound seems to have been aware of the casualties of this development and, to remedy some of them, balanced the latterly conventional "Phyllidula" with the remarkable variety, in tone and theme, of his other early epigrams: *Ladies*, "To Dives," "The Patterns," "Coda," "Epitaph," "Arides," "The Temperaments," "Lesbia Illa," "Three Poets," "To Formianus' Young Lady Friend," "The Bellaires." Further exploration of the genre's expressive potential is seen in his turning to the Palatine Anthology which has preserved for us wholesale so much of the form's scope and early development. As often with Pound it was an indirect turning-to: he began with Florent Chrétien's Latin translation of the Greek and made of it all something of his own, *Homage to Quintus Septimius Florentis Christianus*. It is a fascinating miniature study of Pound's technique and of the rather complicated literary objectives to which he turned translation. In 3, for instance, there is "Propertian" irony and manner in

> A sad and great evil is the expectation of death—
> And there are also the inane expenses of the
> funeral

where "lucri funus inane" gives us the playfully misrendered second line.[3] But the next and final two lines turn away from this jeer at simple sentiment:

> Let us therefore cease from pitying the dead
> For after death there comes no other calamity.

Which is straightforward enough, as K. K. Ruthven tells us:

A few weeks before this poem was published, Pound wrote to Iris Barry telling her that poetry relies on stylistic concision and the presentation of images, but that in addition "one can make simple emotional statements of fact, such as 'I am tired,' or simple credos like 'After death there comes no other calamity.'" (1969, 82)

The combined effect of the second line's irony countered by the level honesty of the third and fourth is an agreeable intellectual and emotional balance and through it a glimmering of the unusual slant of mind that could bring such sentiments into collocation. Consider, too, the deft management of diction in 4 ("Troy") that gives us both a gentle parody of the "ubi sunt" topos that governs the epigram and yet a final, considered endorsement of the spirit of Agathias Scholasticus's original:

> Ὦ πόλι, πῇ σέο κεῖνα τὰ τείχεα, πῇ πολύολβοι
> νηοί; πῇ δὲ βοῶν κράατα τεμνομένων;
> πῇ Παφίης ἀλάβαστρα, καὶ ἡ πάγχρυσος ἐφεστρίς;
> πῇ δὲ Τριτογενοῦς δείκελον ἐνδαπίης;
> πάντα μόθος χρονίη τε χύσις καὶ Μοῖρα κραταιὴ
> ἥρπασεν, ἀλλοίην ἀμφιβαλοῦσα τύχην.
> καί σε τόσον νίκησε βαρὺς φθόνος· ἀλλ' ἄρα μοῦνον
> οὔνομα σὸν κρύψαι καὶ κλέος οὐ δύναται

> Whither, O city, are your profits and your gilded shrines,
> And your barbecues of great oxen,
> And the tall women walking your streets, in gilt clothes,
> With their perfumes in little alabaster boxes?
> Where is the work of your home-born sculptors?

> Time's tooth is into the lot, and war's and fate's too.
> Envy has taken your all,
> Save your douth and your story.

As K.K. Ruthven mentions, "profits" is the result of Pound's (intentionally?) reading "moenera" for Chrétien's translation of τ ε ί χ ε α "moenia"—just the sort of thing that would go into the composition of his Propertius. As would "Time's tooth is into the lot" and slighting anachronisms like "your barbecues of great oxen" for βοῶν κράατα τεμνομένων But the real accomplishment of this modest poem is its turning the language of hard-edged skepticism to encomiastic purposes with reasonable success. And again,there is that lingering sense of subliminal intricacy of mind (the odd pairing of "douth" and "story" gives more than a hint of this) behind the plainspoken locutions.

   Thus in spite of the genre's almost universally accepted formal limitations—"It must have the compression and conciseness of a real inscription, and in proportion to the smallness of its bulk must be highly finished, evenly balanced, simple and lucid"[4]—it is capable of generous measures of suprise. That is to say, while the epigram's conventional focus on a single subject, usually of common interest and in ordinary language, would seem to prepare us for the appreciation of crude effect (of *schadenfreude*, of satirical mirth, or obscenity), we must rather take care to attend to its subtler movements and implications. In his study of Ezra Pound's translations, Peter Schneeman makes this comment on crucial differences between the epigram and Poundian haiku:

> [I]n the epigrammatic poems, the object is social, involving more complex human encounters, so that the further perspective created by the final lines creates a "dance of the intellect" and reveals an ironic intelligence in the poem. This allows the reader to have multiple perspectives, and so to make *judgements* about the object under contemplation—judgements of a kind that are not at all demanded by "In a Station of the Metro." In this latter poem, the depth of the haiku is purely a sensory depth; in the epigrams the depth is intellectual, and depends upon the social or cultural object to create its particular ironic attitude. The experience is fixed not simply as experience, but also as a symbol of the age. (1972, 120)

The presumption of irony is not correct: eulogy, reflection, lament may be all straightforwardly presented in the epigram, Pound's or anyone's. But the emphasis on the interplay between social context and readerly perspective is surely to the point and leads to the further conclusion that an epigram, justly considered, is not always what it first seems. One must "get" more than the "joke." This is certainly true when one reads across the broad spectrum of epigrammatic verse, say, from Archilochus through Simonides of Cos, Callimachus, Meleager, Ennius, and Catullus. But is is more vitally important in reading epigrams, such as those of Martial, which we do not expect to be particularly delicate or subtle. T.K. Whipple, in his study *Martial and the*

English Epigram, falls back upon a dictionary definition of the genre: "a short poem ending in a witty or ingenious turn of thought, to which the rest of the composition is intended to lead up" (1925, 282). But unless we teach ourselves to expect more than this, we, as Eliot did, shall find the poems uninspired and, if not barren, stripped at least of much of their potential delight.

*   *   *

Holding this monition in mind and remembering Pound's punctiliousness in a similar direction, we can turn to Martial, the consummate epigrammatist, and to the phenomenon of his modern English translations. Given the history of the English epigram, flourishing in the sixteenth and early seventeenth centuries (with More, Crowley, Heywood, Wyatt, Kendall, Davies, Herington, Jonson, Guilpin, Bastard . . .),[5] then steadily declining, it is surprising that Martial has found so many modern translators. Responsible for large selections are Paul Nixon (1911), A.S. West (1912), W.J. Courthope (1914), A.L. Francis and H.F. Tatum (1924), J.A. Pott and F.A. Wright (1924), Bohn's Classical Library (various hands, 1926), Dudley Fitts (1956), Rolfe Humphries (1963), Philip Murray (1963), Ralph Marcellino (1966 and 1968), Bariss Mills (1969), Palmer Bovie (1970), Donald Goertz (1971), and James Michie (1972). Among translators of any number of smaller selections are Peter Porter, Peter Whigham, J.P. Sullivan, Brian Hill, Harold Morland, Roy Arthur Swanson. The reasons for such abundance may be several. Perhaps the modern appreciation (until very recently) of obscenity has played a part just as it has with the significant number of uninhibited Catullus translations distilled in the sixties and seventies. Among connoisseurs of the obscene, Martial has a considerable, if somewhat undeserved, reputation.[6] But since the raciest of Martial's work is omitted from a good many of the aforementioned collections, perhaps more pertinent is the very simple fact that Martial was not a modernist. The word has some (albeit anachronistic) relevance. Martial's artistic program, such as it was, amounted to a systematic defiance of the Alexandrian tradition in Greek and Roman verse, especially against the learned mannerisms of Callimachus, Catullus, Propertius, and their imitators in Neronian times. And we need hardly be reminded of the affinities between the Alexandrian legacy—with its metrical experimentation, its learned preciosity, its urbane sensibility—and the discoveries of English modernism. So that while someone like Pound could pick up Martial now and again to learn something about the concurrence of intelligence and plainness of speech, there is bound to be a fundamental inconsonance between the two. On the other hand, a great many (and there were a great many, after all) of those unexcited by the sometimes oppressive flashiness and "perversities" of the modernist movement could turn to Martial or his translations with sympathy. Just as they might turn to the poetry of Robert Graves or others who provided a substantial link between traditional postromantic English verse and the anti- and postmodernists of the fifties to the present. That is not to say, of course, that Philip Larkin's poetry, for instance, is much like translations of Martial but that both, for similar reasons, are unlike the dominant modernists.

It may not be inappropriate, then, that a discussion of Pound's influence on modern translation should at some point touch upon a reaction to that influence. Martial is the appropriate source-language figure and, to begin, the poet-translator must be J.V. Cunningham. "Must be" is perhaps odd. Cunningham, after all, is responsible for only a few Martial translations.[7] But in light of considerations outlined above, he is eminently appropriate. His original verse is conventional in all the old ways; regularity of meters and rhyme enjoy unusual modern prominence as do clarity and precision of diction. Paradox, ambiguity, symbol, and the rest do not wend their difficult and conflicting courses through this verse. To the reader of modern verse weary of the struggle for orientation and certainty, Cunningham's poetry gleams like a warm homestead light in a black Montana nightscape, visible for miles and welcome. But more important still may be the related fact of Cunningham's revival, again in his original verse, of the moribund epigram. His "Century of Epigrams" (1940–69) is a collection of poems founded in good Martialian sensibility but compounded by Jonsonian developments of the genre and finally by Cunningham's own ingenious revisions. The result is a huge range of tone and subject. From the trivial and obscene:

> Lip was a man who used his head.
> He used it when he went to bed
> With his friend's wife, and with his friend,
> With either sex at either end.
>
> (*CP*, 118)

To the humorless sarcasm about the ways of the world we've come to expect from epigram:

> Cocktails at six, suburban revelry:
> He in one corner with the Chest Convex,
> She in another with Virility.
> So they went home, had dinner, and had sex.
>
> (*CP*, 125)

To things altogether more ambitious:

> How we desire desire! Joy of surcease
> In Joy's fulfillment is bewildered peace,
> And harsh renewal. Life in fear of death
> Will trivialize the void with hurrying breath,

With harsh indrawal. Nor love nor lust impels us.
Time's hunger to be realized compels us.

(CP, 115)

Such range is promising. It betokens a conviction that the fulness of experience is susceptible to the hard eye of the epigram and so matches Martial's
conviction when the genre was young and pliant.

On the face of it, then, a more appropriate translator could scarce be
found, and in fact the translations he produces are nearly literal, minor
perfections. No need to fall back on the old sexist saw about translations and
women: lovely and unfaithful or ugly and true. Cunningham translates very
closely, yet with such a sense of the intricacies and dynamics of the Latin and
English that the shift seems effortless and apt. But against all that rightness,
questions will arise. Reading Cunningham is an experience of a different
order from that of reading Martial, and pinning down the disquieting
differences between the two may lead to interesting conclusions. A very
simple example is his version of the oft-translated "non amo te."

> Non amo te, Sabidi, nec possum dicere quare:
>   hoc tantum possum dicere, non amo te.
>
> (1.32)

Virtually everyone knows Tom Brown's famous seventeenth-century version, but I (not unhappy with the obvious) want to use it as a point of
comparison.

> I do not love thee, Doctor Fell.
> The reason why I cannot tell,
> But this I know and know full well,
> I do not love thee, Doctor Fell.

Brown's poem is a topical adaptation of Martial's idea, but one that has
survived beyond its occasion—with unfortunate damage to the memory of
John Fell, dean of Oxford's Christ Church. Its fame, in fact, has surpassed
that of Martial's original, taking on a near-autonomous existence not usual
for translations. But then it's not an ordinary translation; formally, Brown
has turned the couplet into a quatrain with the line breaks at the original's
medial caesurae. The strictly regular effect of the rhyme (not original with
Brown but derived from Thomas Forde who changed Sabidius into
"Nell"![8]), abetted by an equally regular iambic tetrameter, produces lines of
facile effect that virtually leap into one's memory. And the fact that this is
"from the Latin" and has the air of academic gossip about it makes it want to
stay there. Clearly, however, this poem is far from Martial, having none of
the latter's compressed complexity and intricate balances. Does Cunningham
succeed in ways Brown cannot?

> Sabinus, I don't like you. You know why?
> Sabinus, I don't like you. That is why.

In spite of the crude bluntness, one's answer may be affirmative. For one thing, Cunningham's is demonstrably closer to a "translation" than an "imitation" (to revive for a moment that generally useless distinction). Aside from the name changed for metrical reasons and the added "that is why," Cunningham is very near Martial in several ways. His terse phrases mimic the compression of the Latin and allow him to keep to the single couplet—a relatively important consideration since this sort of candid statement works best when not drawn out. Further, Martial's double repetitions, "non amo te" and "possum dicere," are matched nicely enough by repetitions of similar sense units. Finally, Cunningham's rhymed pentameter couplet, weightier in effect than Brown's easy tetrameter, is an appropriate analogue to the elegiac couplet. Both verse forms tend to conclude firmly and decisively.

A reasonably good translation then. But some discomfort lingers. There is in Cunningham's lines an abrasive confrontation that seems not quite there in the Latin—although one might naturally enough expect it in the old, rough and ready tongue. The reason is not far to seek. Both Martial's and Cunningham's "arguments" take the form of tautology, but in the latter case there is a sense that tautology quite properly suffices, that it does in fact constitute sufficient logic: "You know why? That is why." Antipathy needs no defense. But Martial's tautology is vastly more suggestive, implying some of the doubt and irrationality of human disaffection. Whereas Cunningham's exact interlinear corespondences preclude a sense of self-interrogation, Martial's more delicate chiastic pattern of repetition ("non amo te . . . nec possum dicere . . . hoc possum dicere . . . non amo te") suggests a movement from assertion to a momentary reflection about its motives and back, then, to a mildly chastened but still cheerfully frank declaration of unfriendliness. It is a process of consciousness that utterly humanizes this Martial, embodying in the poem that same recognition of passion's hegemony—in spite of our rationalizing efforts—that is found in the almost equally universally known Catullus 85, this poem's clear precursor:

> Odi et amo. Quare id faciam, fortasse requiris.
> Nescio, sed fieri sentio, et excrucior.

The troubling paradoxes here suggest similar tensions in Martial—tensions between reason and unreason, not resolved but recognized and, by Martial, wittily dismissed.

The point is not that Cunningham's translation fails; other translators founder to similar loss on the same shoals:

> I love him not; but shew no reason can
> Wherefore, but this, I *do not love the man.*

Here Rowland Watkyns (17C) is biting enough, but heavy-handed and lacking wit. No sense of Martial's mischief in this. Palmer Bovie's modern version registers more of Martial's subtlety than does either Watkyns or Cunningham:

> Sabidius, I dislike you, but why this is so true
> I can't say. I can only say that I don't like you.

But the poem in this version is not as lively. And although the internal rhymes are rather nice and lend the poem a sense of finish and boundedness, there is no regular cadence in the free verse, dissipating, thus, the poem's original aggressive pungency. Again, my point is not to snoop for failure, nor to expect a single translation to be everything its original is, but rather to note that in any translation the distance and dissonance between model and version is always significant and often (in the best translations) indispensibly suggestive of meaning.

Critics almost always raise the notion that translation must involve an act of interpretation. The translator, like the interpreter, brings what was unnoticed to the fore. Similarly, he neglects some things to make his point. This much is common knowledge. But the analogy between the two activities has further implications. For just as interpretation can never properly exist as an autonomous activity (present fashion notwithstanding), so translation (Zukofsky a case in point) depends in more than obvious respects upon its model. In the case at hand, Cunningham's translation cannot in crucial ways fully signify when considered apart from Martial's original. It is the dissonance between Martial's deceptively subtle "simplicitas" and Cunningham's "up and open" frankness that speaks volumes about both poets. Cunningham's poem alone would reveal less about itself and far less about Martial than we know from seeing them in a kind of Augustinian simultaneity. Of course, translations generally *are* for people who haven't the linguistic background for such comparison, as Nida and anyone with common sense quite properly says. But, on the other hand, they are written by people who do have the necessary background and it may be argued that neither the processes of mind that account for successful translation nor their full suggestiveness can be comprehended unless one can in a sense critically recreate the moment of genesis, when poem and translation exist as a synthetic unity.

Kelly's use of Buhler's categories (reflecting three primary functions of language, "symbol," "symptom," and "signal," as they are called) offers some guidance.[9] On the face of it, Cunningham seems to exemplify what is called a "symbol" approach: literalism, exact transmission of intellectual content. But in the "Non amo te" there has been in spite of this a marked change in "attitude" and one that by being consonant with much else in Cunningham's corpus we can deem intentional. That is, what begins as "symbol" seems to terminate in (albeit subtle) "signal," a departure from literalness and a markedly changed emphasis. But is this all? A slippery poem that won't conveniently fit into its niche? The third and intermediate category, "symptom," appears not (necessarily) to apply; as Kelly describes it, it suggests a sharing, "un don de soi," a personal commitment between translator and translated. To the extent that Cunningham shares a general outlook with Martial and seeks to express that in his translating, this conspiracy of authors might be said to exist, but it is difficult to show—apart from explicit statement by a translator, as Mackenna on Plotinus or Pound, less vividly, on Propertius. If, however, one abstracts the notion of commitment to a textual level, the idea (though perhaps not the term) can be seen to describe the coequal and simultaneously signifying conjunction of the two poems, text and translation.[10] This sharing of function can be, as in Louis Zukofsky's case, explicit, i.e., the translation overtly points to shared sounds, rhythms, and a necessary semantic dependence upon the original:

> Suffenus iste, Vare, quam probe nosti,
> homost venustus et dicax et urbanus,
> idemque longe plurimos facit versus.

> Suffenus is, stay Varus,—whom you've proven—is the
> o most Venusthewed, active ax what, urbane as—
> his damn cue's long reams of preoccupied verses.

Or, as in Cunningham's case, the sharing may be implicit—manifested only in an observable diachronic interplay that points to a more central and complicated textual "dialogue." The process toward or away from literalism is dictated by terms emerging from an acitivity of mind that, perhaps uniquely, is able to cast a "classic" poem into a rare and privileged atmosphere. Within that atmosphere, the original takes on a quality of strange and delicate innocence and becomes for a moment as fresh and young as the translation it begets. The poised balance of the two texts is lost, almost immediately, when the translation is seen as "standing for" its original, or when it is critically pigeon-holed in the usual ways. Translation's happiest and richest moment is its first, when, as in music, theme and variations consort to harmonies grander than those of either alone.

Even in the plainest of epigrams:

> Amissum non flet cum sola est Gellia patrem
> si quis adest iussae prosiliunt lacrimae.

Non luget quisquis laudari, Gellia, quaerit,
    ille dolet vere qui sine teste dolet.

                    (1.33)

In private she mourns not the late-lamented;
If someone's by, her tears leap forth on call.
Sorrow, my dear, is not so easily rented.
They are true tears that without witness fall.

These are poems of no great significance; I choose them only because they are next in each poet's sequence. Again, we see a fairly close translation, the most striking variation being Cunningham's third line, which is a more sarcastic paraphrase. But subtler variances occur throughout and all to a designed end. At the poem's beginning, we note that a more impersonal "she" has been substituted for Martial's Gellia. The effect is quite obviously a greater distancing and the more general applicability of his social criticism. Likewise, the familial reference, "patrem," is replaced by "the late-lamented"—a phrase full of irony and bearing with it the unattractive overtones of modern commercialism and funeral parlor clichés. The commercial motif is maintained in the second line and compounded with sexual innuendo, with the "on call" that translates "iussae," until it becomes dominant in the more drastically revised third line: "Sorrow, my dear, is not so easily rented." Thus what might at first seem to be a word choice dictated by the exigencies of rhyme is, in fact, the culmination of an analogical motif quickly and coherently developed. The notion of "renting" grief, suggesting transience, the secondhand and shabby, and commercial deceptiveness is a perfectly apt metaphor for Gellia's inauthentic sorrow. Equally fitting is the poem's final line—the poet's summary statement—now without any metaphorical burden, but striking in the symmetry of its sound effects: pairs of alliterative words ("they . . . that," "true tears," "without witness") that bind the line together and, with the final rhyme, provide strong closure.

    This is a fine bit of translating. All the effects briefly summarized above are accomplished unobtrusively, while the reader knowing Latin feels that the crucial sense of the original has been successfully transmitted. But the nagging awareness of some dissonance sends us back to the Martial. Martial presents a more personal and immediate situation—"Gellia" rather than "she." Perhaps not a major shift for the translator. But "late-lamented" for "amissum . . . patrem," while also contributing to a more generalized *mise en scène*, signals a more serious change in tone. Martial's situation, with its specific paternal reference, presents a transgression of deeply ingrained Roman values; the ancient centrality of the "paterfamilias" in Roman social and legal codes has some bearing and force even in Martial's jaded imperial Rome. So, while Martial's charge against Gellia is not made histrionically, there is a latent seriousness about it that does not survive in Cunningham's poem. There is also in the Martial no distraction (metaphorical or otherwise) from the particularity of this situation. His third line addresses Gellia with an apparent patience that is most uncharacteristic of Martial and which is not at all transmitted by Cunningham's more detached sarcasm. The result is, in Martial, a willed limitation of rhetoric and irony, a tone of restraint and emotional control. That tone is confirmed in the poem's concluding line—a straightforward sententia which twice sounds the key "dolet." In comparison, Cunningham's version is more cynical, more "wintry" (to use his own term), and flippant—its rhymes even suggesting the effect of highly stylized eighteenth century satire.

The movement represented by this particular act of translation can be traced: a progress is indicated from the specific circumstance to the general, from a note of serious wit to one of cynical levity, from the satire of amelioration to that of broad condemnation. Cunningham's is the next stage in an emotional progress; the perdurance of hyprocrisy, its universality, underscored by the fact that the translation is not so much a restatement of the original but a parallel instance of its burden, virtually cries out for blunter and broader condemnation. The new version *presumes* the old and marks the significant differences between the two. We see, then, that Cunningham's "leap forth" (in "tears leap forth on call") literally invokes Martial's "prosiliunt" (in "iussae prosiliunt lacrimae"), while his choice of "on call" for "iussae" indicates a sharp divergence of tone and implication. The model becomes a necessary backdrop for the new poem, the central bit of remembered history seen, crucially, *as* history.

There is again, then, an observable diachronic interplay. The seeming literality, its closeness to "symbol," becomes an acute register of the translation's subtle insubordination, its "signal," and establishes, in short, the critical relationship of near-difference that in its chronological and intellectual frame makes sense. Making some kind of sense is important—although as we've seen with Zukofsky, it may not be of the sort we expect. One always asks what a translation *does*, even one that seems scrupulously literal: is this Martial? Always, the answer is no. How, then, simply, does one judge it? On one level, by noting, when it occurs, a functional progress born of the coincidence of two worlds and minds—and by marking how that intergerminated progression makes a difference to us. Recall that Benjamin describes translation as a renewal of the original's poetic *intentio*, "not as reproduction but as harmony, as a supplement to the language in which it expresses itself, as its own kind of poetic *intentio*." Thus,

> a translation, instead of resembling the meaning of the original, must lovingly and in detail incorporate the original's mode of signification, thus making both the original and the translation recognizable as elements of a greater language, just as fragments are part of a vessel. (1923, 78)

Benjamin, of course, would achieve this by a close transcription of the words, if not the larger "meaning," of his text. But the suggestive idea is embodied in the image of the broken pieces of the jar, of the complementary nature of the activity. Each piece must fit—whatever its curious dimensions—with the others, and more important, each piece implies another and takes it into account, exists, in fact, in conjunction with it. That conjunction, embodying both contingency and change, is translation's real justification.

A last look at Cunningham and Martial. Here is 4.33:

> plena laboratus habeas cum scrinia libris
>   emittis quare, Sosibiane, nihil?
> 'edent heredes' inquis 'mea carmina.' quando?
>   tempus erat iam te, Sosibiane, legi.

It is a clever and nasty poem that maintains the genial tone of a friendly conversation until the final line. The irony there can turn the poem on its head, making all that geniality a cruel deception. But the ironic final line is susceptible to multiple interpretations suggesting a range of attitude from jaunty persiflage to crushing scorn. Which best applies, or which ambiguity is to be stressed, is the decision a translator must come to. Palmer Bovie's version is nice:

> Your bookcases are crammed with manuscripts
> of the things you have labored to write
> and never bothered to publish. "Oh, my heirs
> will bring out the stuff in due course."
> Isn't it time you published and perished?

A reasonably funny joke in a frame of loose, informal conversation. The distracting humor helps dispel any tincture of cruelty, but the talkative expansiveness points out by contrast the striking concision of Cunningham's version—

> You write, you tell me, for posterity.
> May you be read, my friend, immediately.

—a neat, rhymed, pentameter couplet that, amazingly, compresses Martial's lines without any apparent loss of their ambiguity. The couplet's first line is dense paraphrase, nicely capturing the latent hubris of Martial's poetaster. The second is an almost literal rendition of Martial's closing pentameter. The reader, then, must interpret Cunningham along lines similar to his reading of Martial: a traditional test of "good" translation. Furthermore, the irony in Cunningham's phrasing is cleverly condensed into the crucial "read" placed at the caesura: the homophone comes easily to even the slowest of us. Another nice miniature, capturing, in Benjamin's word, the *intentio* of its model. But just as surely, there is no exact correspondence between the two. Martial's poem leads us gradually to its crushing turn; he dallies, lingering over details and intimating the benign nods and grunts of a sympathetic persona. The effect ultimately is a more startling and piercing deflation. Cunningham forces us immediately to the crux of the issue and prejudices us against his poetaster; one who writes "for posterity" has ego problems. Moreover, his response, with its juxtaposition of "my friend" and an implicit "drop dead," is more immediately and transparently cutting than Martial. So too, Cunningham's jussive subjunctive, more forceful than Martial's indicative mood. There is nothing topical in Cunningham's version to make it definitively a product of its time, but its disgruntled directness, its refusal to bother with drawn out ironies, its sinewy wit, are elements of a distinctly American voice. A voice in sympathy with Martial as he most often is, but not quite the same. As in Benjamin's image, we feel through Cunningham's translation the rough edges of Martial. We may or may not want to read enough of the Latin to go beyond the frontiers where Cunningham and Martial meet. That doesn't matter. What does matter is that they do meet, and that their meeting provokes for us, in us, some further consideration.

Cunningham's poem is then an interpretation and development of certain implications in Martial. And it is precisely this status of revised implication that makes translation a measure of intellectual passage; the distance it records between itself and its original becomes the focus of its being. Cunningham's translations (as minor as these are in the great scheme) are not so much verbal reformulations, as "close" as they often appear to be, but the records of critical intellectual activity. And so we must treat them. We examine the process of translational response; we seek to understand its understandings, motives, goals. When we find that the translation cooperates with its original toward some greater meaning, we call it successful— although that is bad shorthand for our sense of delighted surprise at the revealed richness. Martial's poems ask questions that Cunningham, for his age, answers: this translation, this response, is the right one. We concur; something has come of it. While applauding that rightness, however, we cannot overlook the dialogue it is part of, the interrogation we, also, answer to.

✻   ✻   ✻

L.R. Lind, in an essay full of salutary skepticism, entitled "On 'Modern' Translation," voices considerable discomfort with the "new" sorts of translation sponsored most enthusiastically by the quondam classical journal *Arion*. Lind particularly takes Christopher Logue to task but includes in his critical purview Guy Davenport, Robert Lowell, Robert Fitzgerald, W.S. Merwin, and Louis Zukofsky as well (Janet Lembke, Peter Whigham, and a few others might be seen to fall into the same general category). He objects on three fronts: to translators who don't have well (or at all) the languages they are translating (such as Logue or Merwin); to translations that are so free as to be no reliable guide to what the Greek or Latin says; to translators who, in defense of the above, claim the distinction of being genuine or major poets.

> The example and the precedent of Pope and Pound as translators are still very much with us and will continue to spur the less-than-major poets in the particular genre the latter of the two, at least, represents. In other words, if we do not accept Logue as a major poet (and he has as yet presented no compelling proof that he *is* a major poet) we shall nonetheless be forced to observe more new talents in the field of translation who will, like the inevitable newest and fastest "gun" in the West, attempt to take his place or, at any rate, stand beside him. (1983, 73)

Of course, "majority" is a hard thing to prove or disprove when speaking of contemporaries, and if Pound had waited to get "major" before he did any translating, we should have missed much. But there is no denying that Lind's objection is an important one. The wildest translation is not always the best—in the West or elsewhere. "Best," one asks, for whom? In Cunningham's case, I have argued that the poet (here, one of genuine importance, though perhaps not "major") offers a translation that is a reasonably good guide to what the Latin says. But I have further maintained that what makes the translation distinctive, or shall we say poetically noteworthy, is its collaboration with the original toward something larger and richer than transmission of sense. By which, then, I mean "best" for those who have some idea of what the Latin means and who like to read accomplished verse treatments of it. The Australian, now British, poet and translator Peter Porter, elaborates in commonsense fashion:

> Translating the Classics is, however, less open to doubt than reworking poems from unfamiliar European languages such as Russian, Hungarian, and Czech. The Latin and Greek poets have been read by Europeans for two thousand years. Not only are their poems well-known, both in the original and in many different vernacular versions, but their influence has moulded our own attitude to poetry and even to our own tongue. So there is no danger that the public will get to know a poet in just one version, which may or may not be an accurate recreation of his intent. (1972, ix)

Ideas implicit and explicit here constitute a reasonable response to Lind's general objections, though I think he is wrong in assuming that the Latin and Greek originals are these days "well-known." It may be more accurate to say that they still form an active basis for translational and critical commerce—a commerce that more and more seeks to bring across some understanding of a

work's poetic nature or integrity. Translation at the level of artistic enterprise, and particularly of material that has been so much a part of our
primary literary nourishment, is simply not always to be treated as if the
transmission of semantic "information" were its first purpose.

Further, Porter himself, in his own accomplishment (he does know his
Latin and is an important modern figure), ought to enjoy some credibility
even among skeptics, and it is upon his several translations of Martial that I
want to focus in what remains of this chapter. Such selective scrutiny may
seem a bit arbitrary; the Martials of Peter Whigham, Dudley Fitts, Philip
Murray, and a few others deserve, world enough and time, close attention.
But Porter, like Martial and Cunningham, is something of a traditionalist in
matters poetic and, what is more, a satirist as well. Further, although his
translations will never be on anyone's "must read" list of "major" modern
poems, they *are* interesting as translations and touch upon ideas implicit in
Cunningham's practice while in some senses carrying them further. That in
mind, one might expect a good deal of his renderings. But this?

> Because I don't attempt those modern poems
> like lost papyri or Black Mountain Lyrics
> stuffed with Court House Records, *non sequiturs,*
> and advice on fishing; and since my lines
> don't pun with mild obscenities in
> the *Sunday Times;* nor yet ape Ezra's men
> in spavined epics of the Scythian Marsh,
> The Florentine Banking Scene, or hip-baths
> in Northumberland; nor am I well-fledged
> in the East European Translation Market,
> whose bloody fables tickle liberal tongues;
> despite this I make my claim to be a poet.
> I'm even serious—you don't ask a runner
> to try the high-jump, and if my trade is words
> I'd be a misfit in the People Show.
> From Liverpool to San Francisco, poets
> are turning to the Underground, a pop-
> ulous place where laurels pale. My pleasure
> is to please myself and if the Muses listen
> I may find an ear or two to echo in.

> Quod nec carmine glorior supino
> nec retro lego Sotaden cinaedum,
> nusquam Graecula quod recantet echo
> nec dictat mihi luculentus Attis
> mollem debilitate galliambon:
> non sum, Classice, tam malus poeta.
> quid si per gracilis vias petauri
> invitum iubeas subire Ladan?
> turpe est difficiles habere nugas

> et stultus labor est ineptiarum.
> scribat carmina circulis Palaemon,
> me raris iuvat auribus placere.
>
> (2.86)

It is enough to know that in the Latin Martial is objecting to extravagantly artificial verse making, citing a few examples: "carmine . . . supino" referring to the practice of making the meter read the same, backwards or forwards; "Sotades," the inventor of the elaborate and tricky meter, later known as *versus Sotadeus;* "Attis," from Catullus of course and the fashion (as in Caecilius, Varro, and Maecenas) of making poems on the Attis theme that were notoriously precious in diction and style; and Ladas, a runner of renown who is not supposed to be asked to set out upon the "tumbler's plank." Topical references and necessarily so. Satire finds its victims *there* and points them out. In this case, Martial contemns a popular aesthetic sensibility, the neo-Hellenism that had attained prominence in Nero's circle of poets and remained influential long after. Martial, elsewhere, blames allegiance to its literary god: "Sed non vis, Mamurra, tuos cognoscere mores / nec te scire: legas Aetia Callimachi" (10.4.11–12). The combination of learning and moral turpitude embodied in the manumitted slave, versifier, and grammarian Palaemon is a neat synthetic image of Martial's anathemata here. The theme, tone and language, if not the style, of the poem remind one of Persius's First Satire; naturally enough, as the Martial is a (much) more compact version of the earlier piece.

As is the case with Martial's poem, the texture of Porter's translation is neither elegant nor particularly witty. A tone of off-handed, straight seriousness dominates. Employing the tactics of Johnson's *London,* Porter offers his own topical references—and a relative abundance of them. He makes twenty lines of the original twelve and, accordingly, employs a more discursive style and leisurely cadence. The urgency of his complaint is likewise less acute, and whereas Martial's excorianda are all generally of a piece, Porter's are more diverse—the common theme being servile trendiness of all sorts. But aside from being more numerous and loosely connected, Porter's references are, *mutatis mutandis,* at least as arcane. While a good many allusions are clear enough to provide orientation ("lost papyri . . . Black Mountain lyrics . . . Ezra's men . . ."), some details bewilder. For example, all readers will not immediately recognize precisely in which "modern poems" one finds "hip-baths in Northumberland." Indeed, it doesn't matter that all the references be recognized; the impression that Porter knows well enough that which he dismisses is duly registered. In this, he follows upon Martial's precedent indirectly. In 2.86, Martial displays some of the mannerisms he is criticizing, turning them on their heads; this may be seen is his use of Phalaecean hendecasyllabics (originally an Alexandrian meter), in the greater than usual frequency of allusion, and in the poem's close, its disavowal of the wider public in favor of the privileged few, which is of course notoriously Callimachean. All these devices are turned *against* the kind of verse they are usually associated with. It *is* odd that Martial of all poets should eschew the crowd, the common ear, for the elitism of "raris . . . auribus." So, then, in Porter there is an element of *non sequitur* in:

> Because I don't attempt those modern poems
> like lost papyri or Black Mountain Lyrics
> Stuffed with Court House Records, *non sequiturs,*
> and advice on fishing. . . .

But if we grant that Porter here is undertaking the *kind* of thing Martial has, and has accomplished it in a roughly analogous way, the wildly un-classical nature of his substitutions is apt to throw one off the proper scent. That is to say, one begins to think of this poem not as a translation at all, but as a rather odd, modern programmatic poem. Rather odd, because we don't expect a contemporary poet to talk this way. The oddity is not in his words, but in the logic of his argument, which is originally Callimachean and consequently prominent in the Augustan elegists, Horace, and others as well. The commonness of this type of poem—it is a version of the *recusatio,* the elegists' conventional "refusal" to write on sanctioned topics—is some-thing that a Roman poet would capitalize upon, depending upon instant recognition of the genre and working in slight, ingenious variations. But English poetry after the romantics, while still employing distinctive genres, resists logical mimicry of this sort, works toward more drastic innovation. What Porter gives us, then, is a curious hybrid: an almost painful contempo-raneity wedded to a strictly classical argumentative structure. The notion of hybridizing is, if obvious, suggestive. Diachronic interplay becomes ex-plicit. Strikingly different poetic strains fuse within some single organic composition that has no reason for being anything other than what it is. There is, too, the element of experiment, the same tension of expectation and analysis as when one awaits maturation of a new variety of rose. All this shunts aside an old distinction: translation either exists to transmit data from another language or it seeks to become a poem somehow "in its own right." Porter's translation is decidedly neither, nor tries to be. Rather, in some ways like Cunningham whose translations of Martial he admires, he seeks to represent an antiphone of old and new. The degree to which the two voices conspire to some compositional unity is measured by the extent to which each "makes sense" in light of the other. The English poem, which we have said to be odd, out of place as strictly an original piece, finds a justification in its status as translation. The Latin "voice," embodied implicitly in its foreign logical structure, is redeemed, given meaning and currency, by the audacious contemporaneity of Porter's references and allusions. Elements helpless and incomplete in themselves fuse in fine complementarity to form an aesthetic presence both novel and organically whole.

Yet granting that the poem somehow works is not enough. Analysis explains its oddity but fails to resolve a deeper discontent with (to say it straight) its ugliness. Porter's language is supposed to be plain, of course; that is how one should, in the main, translate Martial. There are no images like those Pound can give us amid his plain talk when he translates Propertius:

"Anienan spring water falls into flat-spread pools"

Pound takes the chance offered by the found image to make, when the occasion suits, beautiful language. Porter has none of beautiful language in his almost oafish demand of the poet's laurel wreath: "I make my claim to be a poet. / I'm even serious." A partial explanation of the tone comes a little later: "My pleasure / is to please myself," followed by an odd qualification: "if the Muses listen / I may find an ear or two to echo in." From Hesiod's famous invocation on, of course, the Muses are supposed to sing, not listen. The inversion is probably further confirmation of the poet's isolation and, more important, of his resignation of lyrical resonances, of conventional cadences, of pleasing sonorities, in short, of that which the Muses generally denote: the "poetic." The Muses are to listen to the man speaking, decidedly not singing, ugly truth, and they must listen because they have somehow gone wrong. Porter's words are poetic only in that abstract sense suggested by Genette when he describes the "margin of silence" about the stream of ordinary or other discourse.[11] Porter's margin of silence requires us to consider his verse poetic, but it is unlike most poetry we know. It offers no compelling images, language, or wit. What it does offer is truth—or Porter's version of that. Which, in turn, leads to further ramifications. In its "truth-saying" Porter's poem translates the essence, but only that, of Martial's perlocutionary burden—its extrinsic effect. Something possible perhaps only in this genre. Satire has always had a unique position in the world of letters. It is virtually always outwardly directed, never a self-contained literary *objet*. It functions tensionally with its real-world audience, as its age-old programmatic images demonstrate—the growling dog of Lucilius and Diogenes, the censor and haruspex of Juvenal, the physician in Persius. So, too, Horace's description of his generic habitat as a frontier and himself as a military colonist is indicative of the notion of the (difficult) commerce between art and life.[12] Only Persius, in his descriptions of the sheer impassivity of the vile world, gives us the strange concept of "self-contained" satire. But Porter, for all the bleakness of his language, is not of Persius's cloth, and his satire on poetry clearly intends to inhabit that frontier be-

tween poem and people, art and life. Its toughness, its rough-clad animad-
versions are a function of that purpose. Porter echoes Martial not in words
but in intention and effect upon his real readers. Only in this sense can he be
said to translate him.

That means, obviously, that he has not tried to resuscitate Martial as so
many translators claim to do, to somehow bring him into modern existence,
but rather to "reenact" him. That is to say, Porter speaks through the
occasion of Martial's poem, takes on the mantle of earlier locution. That, in
one sense, is to ask what it is to "be" a modern Martial—a question with a
myriad of answers and not satisfactorily resolvable apart from a detailed
study of both poets. A shortcut may be of some limited use. Both Porter and
Martial are often programmatically self-conscious, frequently expressing an
awareness of writing among and with and against other poets. Martial's
conspicuous animus against the fashions of antiquarianism and Alexandrian
learning in the verse of his day is echoed by Porter's aversion to the "way
out," as he calls it, and any number of fashions of the poetic moment. But
the respective objects of their criticism matter less than its medium, which,
most generally put, is the darker, satiric voice. And Martial's satire is unlike
that of any of his near contemporaries. It is more artfully contrived than
Lucilius's (see Martial's criticisms of the earlier writer, 11.90.1–4), more
delicately ironic than the high-voltage excoriations of Juvenal and Persius,
yet far blunter than Horace. The key to this difference is his adjudication of
the relation of poem and life. He brings life up against his art: the former to
judge and temper the latter. So, in matters of literary taste, it is what men
really do read that is important.

> a nostris procul est omnis vesica libellis
>   Musa nec insano syrmate nostra tumet.
> 'Illa tamen laudant omnes, mirantur, adorant.'
>   Confiteor: laudant illa sed ista legunt.
>   (4.49)

"Ista" are epigrams, of course. Porter, in his gabby way, translates at length:

> 'What's that you say, everybody likes it,
> buys it, praises it. That's what poetry's about,
> solemn Horror Stories from the Ancient Greek,'
> No doubt, but don't set store by what men praise
> nor what they proudly put on their shelves—
> surprise them reading, it'll be something
> true and scabrous from my kind of book.

Something true and scabrous: Martial, in attending to the actual literary
standards of his audience, is not merely justifying potboilerism. Just as the
manner of ordinary discourse governs the style of epigram, so the rhythms

and features of ordinary life occupy its central focus. This is not a by-product of the satiric impulse, but the assertion of literary value:

> hoc lege, quod possit dicere vita "meum est."
> non hic Centauros, non Gorgonas Harpiasque
> inuenies: hominem pagina nostra sapit.
> Sed non vis, Mamurra, tuos cognoscere mores
> nec te scire: legas Aitia Callimachi.
> (10.4.9–12)

> At tu Romano lepidos sale tinge libellos:
> agnoscat mores vita legatque suos.
> (8.3.19–20)

Martial did not always write in accord with such dicta,[13] but his general observance of them accounts, inasmuch as an abstract description can, for the particular and peculiar quality of his verse—much more so than does his coarseness and obscenity.[14] Porter, while less programmatically explicit, is bound to a similar master. From his "Real People":

> The irascible poet
> with weak eyes
> accuses these reasonable
> faces in the street
> of being merely
> imitations of the perfect
> collection of monsters
> in his heart.
> (149)

Or this:

> It is the little stone of unhappiness
> which I keep with me. I had it as a child
> and put in into a drawer. There came
> a heap of paper to put beside it,
> letters, poems, a brittle dust
> of affection, swallowed by memory. . . .
> ("What I Have Written I Have Written," 286)

Despite the "I" in the last, these poems are not confessional, not at least exhibitionistically so as in Lowell, nor for all their lean spareness are they programmatically anti-intellectual. Rather, we see a complex of cerebral and emotional energy and hear a voice compounded of personal and generic features that ultimately have their ground in ordinary experience. That voice, in the largest terms, maybe "what it means to be" a modern Martial.

But that is too easy. The more precise lineaments of Martial's modernity are best and perhaps only discernible in the translations themselves—where Porter necessarily addresses the question directly. Here is the most translated of any of Martial's works:

> Vitam quae faciant beatiorem,
> iucundissime Martialis, haec sunt:
> res non parta labore, sed relicta;
> non ingratus ager, focus perennis;
> lis numquam, toga rara, mens quieta;
> vires ingenuae, salubre corpus;
> prudens simplicitas, pares amici;
> convictus facilis, sine arte mensa;
> nox non ebria sed soluta curis;
> non tristis torus et tamen pudicus;
> somnus qui faciat breves tenebras;
> quod sis esse velis nihilque malis;
> summum nec metuas diem nec optes.
>
> (10.47)

> Friend and namesake, genial Martial, life's
> happier when you know what happiness is:
> money inherited, with no need to work,
> property run by experts (yours or your wife's),
> Town House properly kitchened and no bus-
> iness worries, family watchdogs, legal quirks.
> Hardly ever required to wear a suit,
> mind relaxed and body exercised
> (nothing done that's just seen to be done),
> candour matched by tact; friends by repute
> won and all guests good-natured—wise
> leavers and warm stayers like the sun;
> food that isn't smart or finicky,
> not too often drunk or shaking off
> dolorous dreams; your appetite for sex
> moderate but inventive, nights like sea-
> scapes under moonlight, never rough;
> don't scare yourself with formulae, like x
> equals nought, the schizophrenic quest!
> What else is there? Well, two points at least—
> wishing change wastes both time and breath,
> life's unfair and nothing's for the best,
> but having started finish off the feast—
> neither dread your last day, nor long for death.

This is a more genial translation than the first and, suiting its matter, an easier read. But Porter's version of this famous poem does share a good many qualities with his other translations. It is obviously more periphrastic than the Martial, in part because, as the translator comments, "the Latin has a much higher specific gravity than the English, and the only way to arrive at the same point is to forget about economy and go for effectiveness" (1979, xii.). The expansiveness also serves to explain:

> I have tried to bring out the point Martial is making faithfully, even if this has led to greater explicitness and underlining than he found necessary. My worst inconsistency has been my use of anachronism. I have kept most of the Roman proper names and many of the Roman places, but freely set beside them such modern terms and references as serve to explain something *quickly* to the contemporary reader. . . . My mixed method may be indefensible theoretically, but I feel that it works in practice. (1979, xi)

So, "friend and namesake" for Julius Martialis explains well-enough the "Martialis" of line 2, and Porter's second line provides a less abrupt introduction to the poem's theme. But some of the English words are there for other reasons; the superfluous "(yours or your wife's)" gives a rhyme to the unobtrusive triplets and an extra twist of wit—so, too, in lines 9, 12, 20, and 23. The rhyme does knit the poem together, however, and circumlocution in its service conspires to effect a sense of relation, boundedness, and economy. But there are other lines whose chief purpose seems to be neither to resolve a rhyme nor to merely explain. These are the "modern terms and references" to which he refers above. These we have seen before, and, as before, they fall into two general types. There is analogy, as in "Town House properly kitchened" for "focus perennis" and "Hardly ever required to wear a suit" for "toga rara" and so on. There is also elaboration, interpolations that add something new to the poem: "nights like seascapes under moonlight" and "don't scare yourself with formulae, like x / equals nought, the schizophrenic quest!" These general translational habits are enlisted under the service of "effect":

> I am well aware that these poems based on Martial are very much re-writings. Ideally, Nabokov's Purity Principle should apply, and I would like to have satisfied myself by avoiding anachronism and vulgarity. But as Nabokov's own example of *Eugene Onegin* Englished shows, fidelity can destroy all poetry in the process. I found, while working on Martial, that in order to reproduce in my own mind the *effect* of his poems I had to employ a range of devices which ran from comedians' jokes to sonorous Keatsean cadences. (1979, x)

Sonorous Keats is rather rare in these translations, but this notion of "effect" we have seen before. What exactly does it signify? Certainly not the lapidary stillness of Rexroth's versions. For example,

> I send you a lock of hair
> From an Arctic race, Lesbia,

> So that you may know how much
> More golden is your own.
>
>   (64)

Rexroth makes four lines of Martial's two:

> Arctoa de gente comam tibi, Lesbia, misi,
>   ut scires quanto sit tua flava magis.
>
>   (5.68)

But there is no expansion or development. Only the impression of quiet, economy, and limit. Instead of which Porter's loquaciousness, though initially less pleasing, aims toward an intellectually more complex goal. He claims to explain, to reproduce poetic effect, and he does so with the resources of the moment. That registers the diachronic, invokes an awareness of history as an active and potent process. Terse quietudes, however like to the character of some Latin epigrammatic verse, fail to suffice. The wash of history requires more audacious responses, and that audacity may take one of two forms. There is sheer defiance, the translation that makes little compromise to the moment—like Milton's Horace C. 1.5. On the other hand, there is complicity—not with an original poet as in Roscommon's "friendship" model of translation but with history itself. Following upon a recognition that the march of time is ruinous to incident and detail, there may be acquiescence and a turning of history's forces to expressive purpose. Thus it is not only that Porter will modernize his references, but that he will do so, as we have seen, with more than acute topicality. The result is that what is often suggested is not a generalized "present," an intelligibility that comprises the instant of composition, of translation, of subsequent reading, but a specific present, which is the moment of translation only. That is another way of saying that there is no intention of "universalizing" this Martial, but rather a focus upon its designed obsolescence. The translational complementarity seen in Cunningham's versions is a consequence of this sort of thinking. Original and translation function together to complete an aesthetic experience that is in part constituted by historical and cultural differentials. Porter's versions suggest a further conclusion. They seem to insist upon partiality rather than hypothesized or sought-after poetic completeness. Poem and translation represent past and present only from the instants of their two acts of expression. Instead of fixing the poem for the nonce and anon, it, precisely, unfixes it. We read what is fading almost from the moment of its composition; there will need to be new explanatory periphrases almost (in the scale of literary time) immediately. Only in two ways does this translation suggest a Bergsonian durée. The first is his mixing of references—"theoretically unsound," he modestly calls it—some classical, some modern. In almost every poem we have an explicit register of *terminus a quo* and *ad quem*. Occasionally, to complicate this a bit, there are verbal reminiscences of other translations: Jonson's version of 10.47, for instance. The second is a logical consequence of the first: if a translation locates itself temporally *vis-à-vis* its original, in some ways bearing towards it, in others away, through its management of internal reference, style, diction, and verse form, it can be said to be, in Aristotelian terms, "an imitation of an action" rather than of an aesthetic object. In the very conspicuousness of the elements of detail that Porter feels he must generate to make the thing new, there is a larger *deixis*—a pointing to the subliminal structures of intent and effect that do, in fact, outlast the decays of history.

The title of Porter's short collection is *After Martial*. The doubleness of its sense is obvious enough. Conventionally, "after" somebody suggests loose translation. The preposition is also a specific marker of sequence, of the orders of precedence and value, of incident and response, action and reaction, of objective and pursuit, and finally of the bare and ineluctable fact of time, of history. Porter's title and the character of his work are evidence enough that the translator is content with his "afterness," that it is his given *and* chosen milieu. Cicero somewhere speaks of "loyalty" to a rhetorical tradition through *memoria*, which he conceives as (in the words of a modern critic) "an active communal faculty to keep history open" (Greene 1982, 64). That is not an unworthy definition, as well, of Porter's sort of translating. Keeping history opens reminds us of Louis Zukofsky and the role of *memoria* in the unusual manners of his translation, but where Zukofsky's obvious loyalty is to text—the sounds of words and their strangeness in a literary frame—Porter's allegiance lies with the praxis of the writer Martial. That loyalty, comprising extravagant revision of structure and detail, a desire to affect a real audience according to the dispositions of satiric epigram, acute evocation of the moment of lived time—is what it might mean to be a contemporary Martial, to enact what Martial enacted.

What that performance implicates is simple enough but transcendently important. It is a calling-back of poetry to the flawed, ugly, and sometimes miraculous world of men and women. There is no tolerance in the words of Martial or his translator for theories of pure and self-referential text. No patience with the kind of verse Stevens emblematized in his "blue guitar." Martial and Porter are, in the Stevensian universe, those singers "of ourselves and of our origins" for whom an "Evening without Angels" is best.

> Bare night is best. Bare earth is best . . .
> Where the voice that is in us makes a true response. . . .

Disjecti Membra Poetae?
Horace, Modern Translators, . . . and Pound

Rome was not better by her *Horace* taught
Than we are here, to comprehend his thought. . . .
—Roscommon

Nam postquam per te patuit, populoque refulsit
Ars Flacci, vatum surrexit vivida proles,
Divinis instructa modis et carmine puro.
—Dryden to Roscommon

It is not enough that [the translator] should wish to help an
ancient civilization survive or to enrich his native language and
literature; he must be trying to enliven and enrich himself. And if
translation or the study of it gives insight into a society's assumptions about literature and life, by the same token the translator
must be a self-critic . . . it is a form of learning.
—Colin Macleod

LEARNING and, again, literature and life. That conjunction has once
more become a chief theme of our engagement with even classical
letters. Much of what we read in Latin and Greek after the "century of
scholarship" that was the nineteenth, we have come to as ordinary and living
readers, simply intrigued by the poetry. Part of that fascination undeniably
stems from the intrinsic strangeness of classical verse. The uncanny lyrics of
Sappho[1] and the quotidian musings of Martial are equally parts and products
of other sensibilities and worlds. With all its ancient vestiges, classical
otherness remains attractive, the more so perhaps with the memory of the
old languages fading progressively from general consciousness. Compelling
as well in a lesser sense may be what Macleod called the "scum and garbage
of criticism" insofar as it outfits itself to make the long journey back so that it
might return with some further bit of something to enable our reading and
discovery. But even in this the poets are our masters: "Critics have to learn
what the poets they read can teach them about poetry."

96

The poet predominantly concerned with teaching was Horace, and perhaps no other has been more closely associated in our times with the edifying
sententia, the instructive tag. Apart from Vergil, no other classical poet is
quoted so much as Horace. But we have not wanted to learn deeply from
him. While Vergil, even among the dead-minded, can hardly fail to haunt, to
touch something, Horace has been relegated to the surface of things. To him
is given the glib tongue—these days. The Renaissance Horace threw down
the gauntlet to Jacob Balde or to Sarbiewski, pagan to (in this case) Jesuits,
and made for fine revisionary poetry—or taught Du Bellay his literary
criticism or found his way into *Titus Andronicus.* The eighteenth-century
Horace dictated a tone—sharp, urbane, satirical, always intelligent—that
gave Pope and the rest their knife-edged charms and their humanity.[2] But the
nineteenth-century Horace rapidly became textbook fodder, practice matter
for schoolboys who, however sure of their paradigms, were simply too
young to have felt much of the poetry or the twistings of mind and soul
behind it. To love Horace then was to have miraculously survived the
deadening drill. The twentieth century finds him old-fashioned, and, in as
much as his image is still the product of the Victorian age, that should not be
surprising. Our time seems to have found Propertius more rewarding, for he
is ingenious, passionate, politically iconoclastic, psychologically exhibitionistic, at bottom a disturbing enigma. Propertius, Donne, Eliot, Pound—
that is a nexus of interrelated sensibility that has dominated our poetic
thinking for three quarters of a century, and we have just begun to shake it.
The first great war of our time killed "dulce et decorum est"; subsequent
wars and genocides have rendered absurd Horace's naïve-seeming political
apologetics. And although we ought to have found sympathy, in our secular
age, with Horace's loose-fitting Epicureanism, we haven't. Maybe we've
wanted to feel our agnosticisms hard won, their recognitions of dramatic
metaphysical vacancies undisguised—as in Stevens's "descending sea of dark"
and Housman's

> Night and no moon and never
> A star upon the night.

To these romantic extravagances, Horace does not answer. Bewildered
enough by the sudden political reorientation of the Roman state, he had little
time for anything beyond the pursuit of wisdom within the natural frontiers
of birth and death.

But in these matters, this perception of Horace, many of us have been
wrong. We have got it wrong because we have done what Horace wouldn't;
we have read our poets carelessly. We have failed to see Horace's subtlety, his
political reservations, his many-mindedness. We have failed to perceive that
his famous sanity was not the product of complacency but of hard work and
thought. We've found Propertius's difficult psyche fascinating, but perhaps

that is because it is so transparent; Horace's psyche, having turned through issues of greater significance, is harder to get to, and most haven't taken the trouble. We've long known of Horace's wit and consummate craftsmanship, but these have become his stigma, indicating to us great absences elsewhere. Ovid's wit manifests "imagination"; Horace's only his "personality." This is not just. It is true that one can only admire the soaring genius, and the tears, of Vergil, but we have let that darken our view of Horace, who in many ways shows us more of ourselves. His versatility of voice is one reason: the coarseness and virility of the *Iambi* or Epodes; the refined and distanced wit of the satires; the relaxed didacticism of the Epistles; the magnificent range and lyrical expressiveness of the Odes.

Ovid, too, was versatile, but his modus operandi seems to have been to take a fixed convention, love elegy or epic, say, and to establish a distance between it and himself, to work often-ironic changes and turns on the old set pieces. That is to say Ovid chose to think not *through* literary convention and topos, but about it. Horace, in this like Propertius, thought through and with the literary conventions he employed. The difference is fundamental. It means that when in an ironic vein, Horace will turn his attention upon human circumstances enacted within generic boundaries; or in an erotic poem, it is to the various postures of the lover—coy, pathetic, comic, resigned—that Horace turns his eye. To put it simply, genre for Horace becomes a means to explore the human temperament. This is true regardless of the literary "kind," or style in which he writes and regardless of the much-discussed stages of his career. And it is, finally, what makes him speak more directly to us than any other classical poet.

But as soon as we are willing to grant that what Horace says is likely still to be of interest to readers today, we run hard against his way of saying it: his use of form and the indissoluble connection between the several lyric meters he employs and his meaning expressed through words. This is a factor of daunting concern in only the Odes, but it is the Odes that we shall be addressing in this essay. It is an old conundrum. Horace claimed to be the first to bring Greek lyric meters to the Latin language. He was not, of course, having been anticipated by Catullus and probably others of the neoterics. But Horace was the first to do so thoroughly, almost systematically, and he drew upon a greater range of lyrical forebears. The neoterics looked to the Alexandrians for inspiration, and there was much to find among them. But Horace preferred to look first to the earlier and more virile strains and manners of Alcaeus and Anacreon and to the delicate subtleties of Sappho. He ranged too across the choral lyric: Pindar, Simonides, Stesichorus, and the rest, plundering from them all meters, themes, images, topoi, manners, words. One result is, obviously, that Horace's meters—Alcaics, Sapphics, Anacreontics, Archilocheans, and several others—are a subject for study unto themselves—particularly in the subtle changes he

worked upon them as he naturalized and personalized them. To say that
these quantitative meters don't work well in English, even when accen-
tualized, is again to belabor what we all know—yet they constitute fully half
of what Horace meant to say. How then *can* Horace speak to us? Is it any
wonder that he seems depleted and anemic in translation? Add to that the
implacable fact that English cannot manage the word arrangement of inflected Latin and the problem becomes multidimensional.

Here is a typical, not awfully ambitious, example of the "tesselated"
Horatian poem, C. 1.23:

> vitas inuleo me similis, Chloë,
> quaerenti pavidam montibus aviis
> > matrem non sine vano
> > > aurarum et silvae metu.
> nam seu mobilibus veris inhorruit
> adventus foliis, seu virides rubum
> > dimovere lacertae,
> > > et corde et genibus tremuit.
> atqui non ego te tigris ut aspera
> Gaetulusve leo frangere persequor:
> > tandem desine matrem
> > > tempestiva sequi viro.

The poem is an easy and lighthearted affair. Imitated from an Anacreontic
model, it is a playful distillation of old themes and images yet still manages to
convey its chief qualities of freshness and charm. Chloë flees the amorous
"Horace" just as a fawn startled by the rustling of leaves or by the sight of a
quick-darting lizard. Does she think him a predatory beast? She must leave
off this childish nonsense and learn to follow a man. The magical effect here
is not that offered by original thought or profound emotion, but rather by a
delicate balance of wit, aptness of image, restraint of emotionalism, a suggestive harmony of "right words," and suitability of accent and form. The
rightness of meter is perhaps easiest to describe: Horace has chosen an
Asclepiad combination, conventionally called the fourth Asclepiad.[3] Asclepiadic meters are simple enough, being built on the choriamb ($-\cup\cup-$)
usually repeated once or twice in a line and introduced in each line by a
spondee. The effect of a typical line is thus of weighty initial stresses that
quickly modulate into a sudden lightness. This is the more true in a fourth
Asclepiad that repeats a basic pattern for two lines ($--\,'-\cup\cup-\,''-\cup\cup-\,'\cup\times$), then
follows with a Pherecratean ($--'-\cup\cup-'\times$, nothing more than a glyconic without a tail, catalectic), and is completed with a full glyconic ($--'-\cup\cup-'\cup\times$). Each
of these types of lines then has a similar fundamental pattern but is resolved
differently, the third line of the stanza particularly abruptly and the fourth
with the satisfying closure the third lacks. The impression of such a prosody

is of seeming unpredictability on the level of word and line within a frame of stability and regularity on a larger scale. It suits very well the quick darting images, fawn, leaves, lizard, within their thematic context of conventional love lyric. But the coincidence of sense and cadence extends well beyond the general character of a meter that trips along in fits and starts; *where* it trips and where it lingers is also telling and almost impossible to describe with any justice to its effect. In the first line, for example, the initial spondee adds weight to "vitas," then, as it were, skips into the fantastic with the ensuing choriamb, "inuleo," then again a strong and long syllable, "me," mitigated by the quick stops of the rest of the second choriamb, "similis." That kind of effect, tedious as it is to describe or read about, is delightful when read directly and properly and is a crucial component of the poem's expressive presence.

Obvious and essential, too, in any Horatian ode is his arrangement of words. Latin's inflected nature allows the words to be shuffled about here and there, (potentially) with extraordinary artistic effect. "Quis multa gracilis te puer in rosa" from C. 1.5 is usually cited as an example, where the pattern of the words on the page represents the maiden, "te," embraced by the slim boy, "gracilis . . . puer," in the bank of roses "multa . . . in rosa." Perhaps Nietzsche's appreciation of these effects can survive another quotation:

> Up to this day I have not had an artistic delight in any poet similar to that which from the beginning an Ode of Horace gave me. What is here achieved is in certain languages not even to be hoped for. This mosaic of words, in which every word, by sound, by placing, and by meaning, spreads its influence to the right, to the left, and over the whole; this minimum in extent and number of symbols, this maximum thereby achieved in the effectiveness of the symbols, all this is Roman, and believe me, elegant par excellence.[4]

In line 23, similar effects, though less dramatic than the line from C. 1.5, can be seen in the first line of the poem quoted above, where "me" at the line's center is unavoidably at the center of the girl's ("inuleo . . . similis") regard. One looks for and finds strategic word placement: "vano" and "metu" at line ends in the first stanza and the polar "matrem" and "viro" in like position in the last. Or, one notes the melodramatic separation of adjective, "pavidam," and noun, "matrem," by the pathless mountains, "montibus aviis"—and a line.

A little poem like this is full of like effects and their analysis could go on for pages, just as could discussion of the deftness with which Horace balances the two "worlds" of fantasy and reality in the poem. Chloë is gently mocked by the poet's likening her to a frightened fawn, and the natural scene he paints is exact and emotionally correct. The fears are natural, primal, and not without darkish overtones: the rustling of brambles and the darting of a lizard are not entirely innocuous. Yet in the middle of it all we find "non sine vano . . . metu" and the obviously playful hyperbole of lines 9–10. The poem concludes, almost with a jolt, in the contrast of the final two lines. Characteristically, Horace closes with a rhetorical figure of sorts, a hyperbaton, thereby allowing "viro" rather than "matrem" literally the last word.

This charming little piece is as simple as any in Horace; a good many are vastly trickier in their use of technique and prosodic effect. This being true it becomes valid to say that an ode of Horace is simply not accessible to reasonable understanding except in its original condition. So little depends on the sense of the words.

> Chloë, you will not venture near,
> Just like a lost young mountain deer
> Seeking her frantic dam; for her each
> Gust in the trees is a needless fear.
>
> Whether the spring-announcing breeze
> Shudders the light leaves or she sees
> The brambles twitched by a green lizard,
> Panic sets racing her heart and knees.
>
> Am I a fierce Gaetulian
> Lion or some tiger with a plan
> To seize and maul you? Come, now, leave your
> Mother: you're ready to know a man.
>
> James Michie

So pale this, and yet Michie has done many of the right things. The metrical irregularity, especially in its use of "short" words, is a pretty effective mirror of the Asclepiads; the rhyme scheme is a "restitution" employed to compensate for the Latin's deeper structural boundedness, unmatchable in the English. Even the tone is generally right—especially in the mock hyperbole of lines 9–10. But for all the good things here, the poem is but a shadow of the other, as English poetic convention must strain its resources to imitate the multidimensional complexities of the Latin. We get the impression of something both light and contrived, and we wonder if it's been worth all the trouble.

But we must thank the gods that poets *have* thought it worthwhile: Sidney, Fanshawe, Crashaw, Jonson, Campion, Herrick, Milton, Dryden, Roscommon, Swift, Pope, Johnson, Cowper, Housman have all given us their tries at it. Some of these, like Milton's *Ad Pyrrham*, have become classics. Others, like Housman's famous version of C. 4.7, are good enough to be reread now and again with real pleasure. And the effort continues. Carne-Ross has in a recent review called Horace the most translated and least translatable of poets—notwithstanding Carne-Ross's having edited for a

number of years the journal *Arion,* which once dedicated a goodly portion
an issue to discussions and translations of Horace.[5] There, one may find an
abundance of worthy and readable (if in some cases now dated) re-creations
by Burton Raffel, Christopher Macgregor, Richard Braun, Tilottama Rajan,
Willis Barnstone and others. Amid such a plenty, we come across this from
Basil Bunting, another from Pound's circle of extraordinary early twentieth-
century poets, C. 1.24:

> You can't grip years, Postume,
> that ripple away nor hold back
> wrinkles and, soon now, age,
> nor can you tame death,
>
> not if you paid three hundred
> bulls every day that goes by
> to Pluto, who has no tears,
> who has dyked up
>
> giants where we'll go aboard,
> we who feed on the soil,
> to cross, kings some, some
> penniless plowmen.
>
> For nothing we keep out of war
> or from screaming spindrift
> or wrap ourselves against autumn,
> for nothing, seeing
>
> we must stare at that dark, slow
> drift and watch the damned
> toil while all they build
> tumbles back on them.
>
> We must let earth go and home,
> wives too, and your trim trees,
> yours for a moment, save one
> sprig of black cypress.
>
> Better men will empty
> bottles we locked away,
> wine puddle our table,
> fit wine for a pope.

    It is difficult to say upon first glance what makes this so distinctively fine.
The appreciations of Cid Corman are entirely just ("This is no exercise; this
is poetry to engage those who are involved in the making of poetry for a long
time yet" [1980, 299].) but clearly won't explain why it works. Nor will
Sister Victoria Marie Forde's pronouncements about the "reflective tone of a
mature and thoughtful persona who speaks with urbane acceptance of the

inevitability of death. . . ." (1980, 310). Earlier in her essay Forde does refer to technique in Bunting's translation, by which she seems to mean craftsmanship and careful use of meter—and that is a good place to start. Horace's C. 2.14 is written in Alcaics, one of his favorite meters, not least for its sonorous effects. Wilkinson's picturesque description is not quite exact in *this* case ("the gathering wave of the first two lines, the thundering fall of the third and the rapid backwash of the fourth" [1945, 152]), but there is at least a headlong quality to the lines within the stanza that militates against end-stoppage until the close of the fourth line which both relaxes built-up tensions with its first syllables and gathers itself finally into a resolved (not in the technical sense of that word) regularity (-ʊʊˈ-ʊʊˈ-ʊˈ-ʊ). Bunting's meter is less predictable—in fact unpredictable line to line—although his stanzas' first three lines generally have four strong stresses and the fourth three in a loose trochaic pattern. But there has been some attempt at finding an analogue to the effect of the Alcaic: no end-stops within a stanza, a sense of resolution and rest at the end of the fourth line that in all but the last strophe concludes with a spondee or trochee.

To compare:

> Eheu fugaces, Postume, Postume,
> labuntur anni, nec pietas moram
>   Rugis et instanti senectae
>   adferet indomitaeque morti;

This read metrically conveys inevitability in its first two lines, impending darkness in all the longs of the third, and a hurrying, almost precipitous resolution in the fourth.

> You can't grip years, Postume,
> that ripple away nor hold back
> wrinkles and, soon now, age,
> nor can you tame death.

Here the free verse is used to a conscious purpose. Horace has the "years slipping away" ineluctably; the passage of the metric unit, inevitable and predictable, is the exact analogue to passing time. It is precisely "in control." Bunting changes the subject of the sentence and the point of view: "*you* can't grip years . . . nor can you tame death." Stressed and unstressed syllables come willy-nilly (seemingly) and the burden of that is certainly that thus go the vicissitudes of fate and time. Look closer to the workings of the stresses, accents that slow the line ("yŏu cán't grip yeárs"), then lose hold ("Pós-tŭmĕ"). Again, "nŏr hóld báck / wrinklĕs aňd sóon, nŏw, áge." If technique is the systematic application of poetic resources on a variety of levels (not merely that of feeling, as so often in modern poetry, but lexical, syntactic, prosodic, formal), there is some sophistication of technique in Bunting's translation. That's particularly interesting *in* translation since one must search out a series of analogues to the technical devices of the original and harmonize them, a feat often as complicated and difficult as (perhaps more so than) imitating the Latin meter in the English. Bunting seems to manage this. Four-line stanzas, a "metrical presence," an equivalence of "linkage," line to line, so that there is something like a similar clausular rhythm between the two, the pauses and emphases falling where they should—these things have been thought through.

Premeditated, too, seems to be Bunting's management of language on lexical and syntactic levels. As in Horace, there is an inhering boundedness, an inscape, in these English stanzas as well as between them—in spite of what Bunting once had said:[6]

> Horace works wonders with a word order which was crabbed to his contemporaries, as one may see by reading Lucretius and Ovid on either side of him in time. It is not right to banish such effects, which have their place, one I think too much neglected now, even though we and especially I follow Yeats' example of plain diction and plain syntax.

There may be some irony in that. Bunting has not in his translation gone in for full-scale word patterning, but he has attempted the interconnectedness it accomplishes through other means. As in the third stanza:

> giants where we'll go aboard,
> we who feed on the soil,
> to cross, kings some, some
> penniless plowmen.

The interlacings are plain enough: "where we'll go aboard" (Charon's raft, of course, and just as elliptically in Horace); then, "we" explained in an hypotactically suspended clause; then, "to cross" (the river Styx, antiphony of earth, "soil," and water made explicit)—"kings some, some" (velars, sibilants, repeats)—"penniless plowmen" (closing alliteration and back to earth and dust). Reticulated patterns of lexical and phonic elements, internal rhyme, alliteration, semantic echo ("seeing," "stare," "watch"), and, in the penultimate stanza, jumbled connectives and adversatives that heap and unheap things not quite randomly:

> we must let earth go and home,
> wives too, and your trim trees,
> yours for a moment, save one
> sprig of black cypress.

The "trimmed" and bare simplicity of "sprig of black cypress" then governs the tone of the final stanza—rendered with lucidity yet capturing all of Horace's quiet and almost bitter irony.

> absumet heres Caecuba dignior
> servata centum clavibus et mero
> tinget pavimentum superbo,
> pontificum potiore cenis
>
> Better men will empty
> bottles we locked away,
> wine puddle our table,
> fit wine for a pope.

Bunting has written with Poundian dogmatism. "Poetry used to be written to a tune; beware, however, of trying to reproduce its meter" (1936, 714). But there is something of tunefulness in this translation and more than a little attention to meter. Rhyme is supposed to be out: "Rhyme itself is a handicap, fatal to the classics" (1936, 714). But of internal rhyme there is a plenty in Bunting (as there is in the Latin) and a cognate relatedness among elements that makes this something *like* rather than only a translation of Horace.

That is to say, Bunting, demonstrably here, learns from Horace, is compelled to experiment with English resources to find some analogue to Horatian technical sophistication. The result is finer poetry—and the same is true to a lesser degree of the other translations quoted above. It is certainly true of Bunting's earlier Horatian translations, which veer much more wildly from the literal sense of the Latin.

> Yes, it's slow, docked of amours,
>   docked of the doubtless efficacious
> bottled makeshift, gin; but who'd risk being bored stiff
> every night listening to father's silly sarcasms?
>
> If your workbox is mislaid
>   blame Cytherea's lad . . . Minerva
> 's not at all pleased that your seam's dropped for a fair sight
> of that goodlooking athlete's glistening wet shoulders
>
> when he's been swimming and stands
>   towelling himself in full view
> of the house. Ah! but you should see him on horseback!
> or in track-shorts! He's a first-class middleweight pug.
>
> He can shoot straight from the butts,
>   straight from precarious cover, waistdeep
> in the damp sedge, having stayed motionless daylong
> when the driven tiger appears suddenly at arms'-length.
>
>   (CP, 128)

Which poem, as Forde has commented, works very hard to find a reasonably fixed metric correspondence to the odd (even for Horace) "ionic a minore" of the original, *C*. 3.12:

> Miseram est neque amori dare ludum neque dulci
> mala vino lavere, aut exanimari metuentis
>   patruae verbera linguae.
> tibi qualum Cythereae puer ales, tibi telas
> operosaeque Minervae studium aufert, Neobule,
>   Liparaei nitor Hebri,
> simul unctos Tiberinis umeros lavit in undis,
> eques ipso melior Bellerophonte, neque pugno
>   neque segni pede victus:
> catus idem per apertum fugientis agitato
> grege cervos iaculari et celer arto latitantem
>   fruticeto excipere aprum.

The Latin has two very long, very regular lines followed by an equally regular octosyllabic, no substitutions. Bunting uses one (broken) long and two shorter lines and manages to give something of the Ionic feel (∪∪−−) (Forde 1980, 309). Established formal boundaries generate strength: Horace's old lesson. But it is *within* those limits that virtuosity appears—in this case through Hopkinsian sound effects (to go with the Hopkinsian long line?), right down to the "Ah!" And that in turn is wedded to an offhanded tone that is pure Bunting—common, sensuous, frank. The governing theme, the plain eagerness of sensuality, in large measure (apart from bits of fun like "pug" from "pugno") accounts for the anachronisms and modifications ("aprum" to "tiger," for instance).

Of course, pertinent in all this are Bunting's ideas on how translation ought to be done, expressed just about as dogmatically as Pound's: to translate not "sentence by sentence" or "effect by effect" but "nothing less than the whole poem . . . disdaining fidelity to any mere part" and to preserve "idiom in the sequence of ideas" (1936, 715). That's well enough, though not so terribly illuminating. More to the point, Bunting knows of translation and poetry through translation; and Horace is the teacher: "If ever I learned the trick of it, it was mostly from poets long dead whose names are obvious: Wordsworth and Dante, Horace, Wyat and Malherbe . . ." (*CP*, preface). From which one ought not simply to conclude that the best translator-poets are those who attend to stodgy things like form and meter because that is what the old crowd did, that therefore the "metrical" translations of Horace by J. B. Leishman and Charles Passage and, to an extent, Michie are what one should aim for. Or that modern poetry in general ought to go about finding something to replace the Pound-broken pentameter—though it might. But perhaps quite the contrary. Translation, that artificial situation wherein one faces most directly what Harold Bloom calls the "strong" precursor, creates a pressure that can be either responded to or avoided. Most, worrying about whether one should or should not literally translate what the original "says," escape it. Some few others are compelled to a strong reaction that is finally not so much revisionary as creative. But not merely that. Steiner's multistage process, Kelly's elaborate analytical descriptions, Nida's system of correspondences between source and target languages, Dryden's "paraphrase," and most of our other secondary and theoretical descriptions amount to schematic boundaries within which intensely creative activity occurs. There is no objective analogue to Horace's syntactic complexities in English; those who take up the challenge of translating and who don't abdicate the hard part find some sufficient reply, fully as difficult and as rewarding.

That may not mean contriving an ad hoc substitute that resembles "Ionic a minore"; it may mean making this out of neat second Asclepiadic couplets:

> Please stop gushing about his pink
> neck smooth arms and so forth, Dulcie; it makes me sick,
> badtempered, silly: makes me blush.
> Dribbling sweat on my chops proves I'm on tenterhooks.
> —White skin bruised in a boozing bout,
> ungovernable cub certain to bite out a
> permanent memorandum on
> those lips. Take my advice, better not count on your
> tough guy's mumbling your pretty mouth
> always. Only the thrice blest are in love for life,
> we others are divorced at heart
> soon, soon torn apart by wretched bickerings.
>
> (*CP*, 129)

The Horace, C. 1.13:

> Cum tu, Lydia, Telephi
> cervicem roseam, cerea Telephi
> laudas bracchia, vae meum
> fervens difficili bile tumet iecur.
> tum nec mens mihi nec color
> certa sede manent, umor et in genas
> furtim labitur, arguens
> quam lentis penitus macerer ignibus.
> uror, seu tibi candidos
> turparunt umeros immodicae mero
> rixae, sive puer furens

> impressit memorem dente labris notam.
>   non, si me satis audias,
> speres perpetuum dulcia barbare
>   laedentem oscula quae Venus
> quinta parte sui nectaris imbuit.
>   felices ter et amplius
> quos irrupta tenet copula nec malis
>   divulsus querimoniis
> suprema citius solvet amor die.

The justice of Bunting's reaction in formal and lexical terms is confirmed by a complex but valid reasoning. Horace's poem derives obviously from Sappho 31—and from Catullus's translation, poem 51. But R. G. M. Nisbett and Margaret Hubbard are surely right in noting that it is influenced by similar treatments of love's or jealousy's pathology in Alexandrian epigram where the intent is far from the emotional soul baring in Sappho. The conflation establishes distance and irony, and the use of the relatively lightweight Asclepiadic couplets and occasional colloquialisms confirms it.[7] But the final stanza changes registers once again, and we have something like a serious statement on the nature of love. This is complex enough to make merely reading the poem something to be approached with care. The translator might choose couplets to express the kind of distance Horace is implying, but to do that would be to overly formalize that which should sound casual and ironic. Bunting instead does what Pound often does with Propertius, boils him down to disillusioned tonalities of careless statement. He runs through the catalog of symptoms ("makes me sick, / badtempered, silly: makes me blush. / Dribbling sweat on my chops proves I'm on tenterhooks") as one quite a lot bored with the whole thing. Thirteen (albeit longer) lines to translate twenty—and *Latin* is supposed to have the high specific gravity. The cadences and language are those of the plainest talk, stresses jumbled now here now there, line breaks where one might take a breath if one didn't much care about syntactic continuity ("pink / neck") or did subliminally care about something ("permanent memoranda on / those lips"). Systematic irregularity of form here is one right way to put this plain man's "secondary" rhetoric and at the same time to turn the trick at the end and make a serious assertion about love. Bunting in doing this last thing inverts Horace's intention, allying his persona with the "divorced at heart" rather than with thrice blest true lovers. But even that echoes Horace's gesture: Horace amending Alexandrian ironies with a contemporary Roman ideal; Bunting turning the coin up again to a modern realism—"soon, soon torn apart by wretched bickerings."

That this is an essentially technical response to the Horatian poem rather than just another example of vers libre slackness may be seen indirectly, through a quick look at Bunting's translation of Catullus 51, one of Horace's models for *C.* 1.13:

> O, it is godlike to sit selfpossessed
> when her chin rises and she turns to smile;
> but my tongue thickens, my ears ring, what I see is hazy.
>
> I tremble. Walls sink in night, voices
> unmeaning as wind. She only
> a clear note, dazzle of light, fills
> furlongs and hours
>
> so that my limbs stir without will, lame,
> I a ghost, powerless,
> treading air, drowning, sucked
> back into dark
>
> unless, rafted on light or music,
> drawn into her radiance, I dissolve
> when her chin rises and she turns to smile.
> O, it is godlike!

That, with its clear imitation of Catullus's Sapphics, its careful control of diction and phrase, rhythm and tone, so that the effect is almost more like Sappho's delicate seriousness than Catullus's artful revision, is what Bunting can do with much the same kind of thematic material. And when the pressure applied by the original requires another kind of reaction. In all of these instances, the Latin provides not only a model for Bunting to work on, not only a message to rephrase, but some crucial stimulus to the modern poet's technical artifice. Horatian metrical virtuosity, its mosaic cohesiveness, its love of contrast and surprising turn—all find their analogues in *Briggflatts* and Bunting's two books of *Odes.* The relation may be coincidental. Probably not.

The same issue of *Arion* that was the forum for some very good translations of Horace reprints, conveniently, Ezra Pound's well-known 1930 essay on Horace and his translators.[8] It is a masterpiece of the kind of thing Pound is famous for: spouting trenchant understandings and wild misunderstandings with equal and enthusiastic dogmatism. It is too a good measure of his earlier ambivalent attitude to Horace, expressed in colorful quotables:

> Quintus Horatius Flaccus, bald-headed, pot-bellied, underbred, sycophantic, less poetic than any other great master of literature . . . a liar of no mean pomposity . . . lifts passages, incorporates lines; I doubt if he improves on Alcaeus. . . . Horace at his best is sometimes more, some-

times less than a translation. . . . Against the granite acridity of
Catullus' passion, against Ovid's magic, and Ovid's sense of mystery,
Horace has but a clubman's poise and no stronger emotion than might
move one toward a particularly luscious oyster. . . . Unless someone
really were "a Horace" I see no chance of a real translation. . . . It is
difficult to imagine anyone wanting to feel like Horace with sufficient
force to produce the equivalent idiom.

And while there is no denying Horace his fans in classics departments,
Pound here dictates an important statement of literary taste. So much is this
so that when a poet—Auden, for example—is generally deemed Horatian,
that is because he is seen by most to have resigned major poetic ambition, to
have settled for the small thing. Yet in the same essay, Pound did put his
finger nearer the pulse of Horatian virtú:

> But there is definitely Horatian art. Apart from Catullus, he was the
> most skillful metrist among the Latins. . . . [He gives pleasure] to the
> connoisseur by his verbal arrangement. . . . This literary pleasure is not
> due to the passion of Horace, but to the order of words and their
> cadence in a line measured by the duration of syllables. ("Horace," 217–
> 18)

A good deal *can* be made of this, more certainly than the impression that
Horace was to Pound merely a soulless technician. There is in these opinions
the same tendency to see in a poet's literary leavings qualities of human
personality that inspire affection or aversion as in his view of Propertius and
Cavalcanti. One sees again too the "need" for interfusion of personalities of
poet and translator. Apparent further is the influence of Pound's reading of
Propertius and his appreciation of the elegist's anti-Augustanism, an attitude
Horace did not so clearly share. Then there was the war and "non 'dulce,'
non 'et decor.'" But the first two of these observations have general and
technical pertinence only—pertinence to Pound's manner of approach in
imitating, translating, other poets. As for the rest, Pound's "aversion" to
Horace—that should be handled with care and treated as the literary criticism it is, showing that Pound's reading of Horace was a complex and mixed
one, rather than any kind of privileged psychological testimony.[9]
    In that light, the essay is at least a very good bench mark indicating the
quondam critical distance Pound maintained with respect to certain features
of Horatian art. Those features are, as Pound saw them, at least these: an
emotional coolness, heterogeneous thematic texture to the verse, "matter
which is not direct presentation of objects, or even direct statement of
anything," an imagination of subdued rather than conspicuous contours,
and, more generally, the inability to inspire "untempered admiration." Some
of these objections are based upon careless misreadings, and others, founded
in the aesthetic criteria of the moment, were bound to change. Mundus

senescit; and there were for Pound, in the thirty-odd years intervening between the 1930 *Criterion* essay and his remarkable Horatian translations of 1963 and 1964, dramatic, even traumatic occasions for personal, intellectual, and artistic reevaluation. The best index to the last may be the translations themselves. The first, C. 1.11:

> Ask not ungainly askings of the end
> Gods send us, me and thee, Leucothoë,
> Nor juggle with the risks of Babylon,
>   Better to take whatever,
> Several, or last, Jove sends us. Winter is winter,
> Gnawing the Tyrrhene cliffs with the sea's tooth.
>
> Take note of flavors, and clarity's in the wine's manifest.
> Cut loose long hope for a time.
> We talk. Time runs in envy of us,
> Holding our day more firm in unbelief.
>
> Tu ne quaesieris, scire nefas, quem mihi, quem tibi
> finem di dederint, Leuconoë, nec Babylonios
> temptaris numeros. ut melius, quidquid erit, pati,
> seu pluris hiemes seu tribuit Iuppiter ultimam,
> quae nunc oppositis debilitat pumicibus mare
> Tyrrhenum: sapias, vina liques, et spatio brevi
> spem longam reseces. dum loquimur, fugerit invida
> aetas: carpe diem, quam minimum credula postero.

If this is not the best known of Horace's poems, it contains his most famous phrase; yet it is much more than a collection of conventional Epicurean pieties. "Pieties," however, may be the right word, for although it is a drinking song with amorous overtones, there is something simply serious about the poem, a straight accounting of human purpose, place, and joy. It, while modeled on epigrams of a known type, has nothing of empty conventionality in it; there is honesty, yet freshness and light. The greater Asclepiads help: the choriambs dance along three to a line, the length and steadiness of which brings something of dignity. Pound, after Marvell and Herrick and Donne, might have treated this far differently than he has. One can imagine him in the spunky mood of the *Criterion* essay rendering an awful parody of the poem, the chubby gentleman's cooing lust "seizing the day" in one of Pound's better dialect voices. But instead he has given us this quiet, lovely thing. The bit of old-fashioned English may even send us back to Pound's very early translations ("O Lady mine, doth not thy sight allege / Him who hath set his hand upon my heart") and we may wonder whether he has gone "straight" or back. But the archaism is slight after all and is there for a good Poundian reason (homophonic: "quem mihi, quem tibi"), and the rest of the poem does other things Pound used to do: rephrase or misconstrue ("juggle with the risks of Babylon" for "Babylonios temptaris numeros"); rearrange syntax ("several or last, Jove sends us. Winter is winter."); turn things around (Pound has the sea gnawing the cliffs, while Horace has rocks working away at the sea); overliteralize ("take note of flavors" for "sapias"—how good that is!); extrapolate ("and clarity's in the wine's manifest" for "vina liques"); eliminate what had become cliché ("Holding our day more firm in unbelief" for "carpe diem"). So it is Pound, after all.

But like his friend Bunting, Pound has turned the pressure of Horace's formidable artistry toward some richly worked English presence. Perhaps that is most surprisingly seen in the poem's form; which is a nigh-regular curtal sonnet, broken at precisely the right point, where tone, register, and "landscape" changes. Here too are Horatian interlacings Englished:

> Ask not ungainly askings of the end
> Gods send us, me and thee, Leucothoë;
> Nor juggle with the risks of Babylon,
>   Better to take whatever,
> Several or last, Jove sends us.

But then not forgetting himself,

> Winter is winter . . .
> We talk. Time runs in envy of us.

Internal rhymes, the linkage of repetition, the expressive and conscientious use of free verse—the usual things in Pound and things he didn't need Horace to tell him about but used to a consummate perfection in this little ode because Horace used *his* art that way.

But there is another piece to this puzzle beyond care with words and form, and it has to do with *what* Horace says. Pound begins, "ask not ungainly askings" and turns us back through Hemingway and Donne to Horace who said the thing first. There is honor paid in the line, and humility rendered, here and in the quiet restraint of the verses and in "Cut loose long hope for a time," which brings us back to the Pisan "Pull down thy vanity" and the issue *that* turns on: "Learn from the green world what can be thy place in scaled invention and true artistry." But to contrive true artistry around what Horace has written, what searing time has colored as a series of commonplace nostrums, gives occasion for wonderment. Either the pleasures and consolations of the moment as against the effluxions of time have come to *matter* to Pound more than the great themes of history (which is to say that garden-cultivating *ataraxia* has come to signify more and better than those ideas which obsessed the man throughout the Cantos), or his old preoccupations, in translation, have been artistically sublimated, even transformed. Remember "the granite acridity of Catullus' passion" and "Ovid's magic, Ovid's sense of mystery," both of which "add something to world poetry," and remember too Propertius's passion, his startling imagination, his anti-Augustanism, and finally Pound's own passions that he felt could bring his far-flung poem, the Cantos, together. But that center didn't hold, as the final fragments acknowledge: "I cannot make it cohere, . . . I cannot make it flow through." The admission (and its qualifications: "It coheres all right / even if my notes do not . . . to confess wrong without losing rightness") is important insofar as it touches not only moral values, but aesthetic values as well, there never being a real separation of the two for Pound. Not passion, then, but something else—coherence. And it is the submission of passion to patterns of coherence that he offers in the three last Horace translations.

The central fact then is that these translations constitute something like Pound's last programmatic statement about poetry. The choice of translated poems is evidence enough: C. 1.11 is one of Horace's best-known and finely presented apologies for an Epicurean sensibility, which in a Poundian context assumes a relevance to the life and values of the poet. The second translated ode, C. 1.31, is, in almost perfectly consequent logic, the poet's declaration of identity and purpose, occasioned for Horace by the dedication of the temple of Apollo in 28. C. 3.30, which Pound renders last, is the most famous celebratory closure in the history of poetic art. The translations together say something in the spirit of "artem virumque cano," and Pound surely means that they should. Precisely *what* they say is more difficult to ascertain since that is not simply what Horace has written but, as with the Propertius, some synthesis of what Horace and Pound together signify—a conjoining of intentions that is crucially other than the sum of its two parts.

It is best to begin again with C. 1.11. Horace's poem starts conventionally with a statement so general that it could be called either Epicurean or Stoic: It's not right to seek to know one's end or fortunes in advance; better simply to bear what is bound to be. Then, a sentence of astounding and delightful incongruity:

> seu plures hiemes, seu tribuit Iuppiter ultimam,
> quae nunc oppositis debilitat pumicibus mare
> Tyrrhenum.

"Hiemes" is of course synecdochic for a more general sense of passing seasons and time but also bears the traditional valences of poetic "winters." Easy enough. But then the poem trips itself up; the "mare Tyrrhenum," another traditional figure for time, instead of slowly eating away at the rocks against which it crashes, is itself worn down by the rocks. Surely water consuming stone, a trope dating from the pre-Socratics, is one of the oldest

of conventional images, so the inversion is a surprise. It gets more complicated as the subject of the verb "debilitat" is "quae," relative to "ultimam,"
i.e., the "last" winter. Do the tropes work merely against one another? Time
defeating time in what one commentator calls a "cumbersome" figure?
Another look and the thing takes on a slightly different color. Surely the sea's
water does erode the cliffs of land—they but appear to break futilely apart
on the stony mass—or rather they do different things in respective temporal
contexts we'd call "human" and "geological," the same general distinction
hinted at in "spatio breve / spem longam reseces." The turnings of figure,
being both false and true, true and false, shift the poem into another register
in which it is fair to say that one can resist time and that one cannot. It all
depends. By "straining the wine" and abandoning long-term plans one
becomes much like "oppositis pumicibus," and so, "fugerit invida aetas."
But equally, envious time is a-wasting "dum loquimur," and what needs to
be done is some good, short-term embracing of life's opportunities. But then
again that is to try to possess (surely denoted by "carpere") that which is
most fleeting, time itself ("diem"). Rather than being merely an exhortation
to enjoy the day (though it is *at least* that), the poem suggests a relation
between humanity and time that is essentially problematic, that shifts with
perspective and offers no easy and fully satisfying resolution. The dimensions of the thing waver, as if at a great distance: we know what it *should* be,
a simple Epicurean desideratum, but that is not quite what we see.

This shifting and deceptive matrix of human relation to time is the locus
within which Pound is to work through the problem of artistic coherence—
that is to say, to think it through in a historical frame whose chief feature is
the disintegration of constructed wholes, even the "basic sense" of a poem.
Pound begins, deceptively, with the kinds of translator's choices that reflect
Steiner's brand of critical incursion and restitution. "Ungainly" surely stands
in secular place for "scire nefas" and marks a transition from a system of
cosmic interdiction and influence to one chiefly ethical (in the root sense), a
condition wherein "manners" do matter: to ask ungainly is to lack the grace
of simple human dignity. "Juggle with the risks of Babylon" equally slights
eschatology, and "Jove" is a cipher here whose timing is not to be depended
upon. Pound's "winter" is more neatly "death" than Horace's, or mortific
time straightforwardly "Gnawing the Tyrrhene cliffs with the sea's tooth"
(recalling, of course, "time's tooth is into the lot"). All this amounts to a
pulling in, a constriction of Horace's more rambling figural possibilities.
And that is as translation often works, critically selecting and limiting. As
fine as it is, line 6 avoids Horace's pivotal inversion of figure upon which
depends so much of the poem's spark and puzzle. Is he setting out to shun its
"ungainly" questions? The transferred epithet, "Tyrrhene," and the entirety
of line 7, pivotally placed at the sonnet's break, reassure us that Pound has
read *through* Horace's figures: "winter" is a broken-toothed old man,

"gnawing" relentlessly and endlessly, effective finally, but dessicated and inert in all but merely material terms. Then the sonnet's shift, which is a mirror to Horace's inspired figure: "Take note of flavors, and clarity's in the wine's manifest." The counter is to the tasteless gnaw of deadening time and to Horace's "sapias": "wise up" is the Latin's most obvious sense, but Pound's hyperliteralism is a strong metaphoric redirection. So there is chewing and there is tasting, but the vivid gustatory element, its strictly vital aesthesis, is inadequate alone (although we know the figure is already loaded, wine and poetry locked together since "The Amphora" in 1908). "Take note . . . clarity . . . manifest": there is in Pound's line not merely perception, feeling, sense, but the involvement of a clarifying, ordering consciousness. That in turn is the essence of "We talk" which without the Latin's subordinating "dum" assumes, in the independent English clause, the character of organizing intellectual activity and hence a prominent importance. "Dum loquimur, fugerit invida / aetas"; talk for Horace is dilatory, a waste of time; for Pound it is that which "for a time" places one out of the flux: "time runs in envy of us." It is the moment of aesthetic perception, then, attended by intellect's "clarity," that signifies human resistance to time's tooth. It is of course a resistance of only a moment, a matter of present tense in verb and participle. "We talk . . . holding. . . ." Finally, "in unbelief"—here having not much to do with religious conviction, but with the temporal proposition implicit in the English participle. And that is as Horace has it: "quam minimum credula postero." The moment coheres and so the poem, and that complexly enough to demand the fixity of attention.

This is a point of beginning. It announces the terms within which Pound will say more explicit things about poetry in the next two translations. The first of these is from C. 1.31:

> By the flat cup and splash of new vintage
> What, specifically, does the diviner ask of Apollo? Not
> Thick Sardinian corn-yield nor pleasant
> Ox-herds under the summer sun in Calabria, nor
> Ivory nor gold out of India, nor
> Land where Liris crumbles her bank in silence
> Though the water seems not to move.
> Let him to whom fortune's book
> Gives vines in Oporto, ply pruning hook, to the
> Profit of some seller that he, the seller,
> May drain Syra from gold out-size basins, a
> Drink even the gods must pay for, since he found
> It is merchandise, looking back three times,
> Four times a year, unwrecked from Atlantic trade-routes.
>
> Olives feed me, and endives and mallow roots.
> Delight had I healthily in what lay handy provided.
> Grant me now Latoë:

Full wit in my cleanly age,
Nor lyre lack me, to tune the page

Quid dedicatum poscit Apollinem
vates? quid orat de patera novum
    fundens liquorem? non opimae
        Sardiniae segetes feraces,

non aestuosae grata Calabriae
armenta, non aurum aut ebur Indicum,
    non rura quae Liris quieta
        mordet aqua taciturnus amnis.

premant Calena falce quibus dedit
fortuna vitem, dives et aureis
    mercator exsiccet culullis
        vina Syra reparata merce,

dis carus ipsis, quippe ter et quater
anno revisens aequor Atlanticum
    impune. me pascunt olivae,
        me cichorea levesque malvae

frui paratis et valido mihi,
Latoë, dones, et, precor, integra
    cum mente, nec turpem senectam
        degere nec cithara carentem.

In the best sense, Pound's version is transitional and can be so discussed. The Horace is a priamel: after a series of counter examples, the poet self-consciously comes to a declaration of that desire or way of living which pertains specifically to him. Pound in translating follows a conventional course, although his syntax in the first few lines is a bit denser. In answering Horace's rather matter-of-fact tone (surprising, for so august an occasion), Pound's prosaism, "specifically," is good. But the commerce between this poem and its original is at least matched by its linkages with his version of C. 1.11. Pound closes his first strophe with an image that picks up obvious themes: "Land where Liris crumbles her banks in silence / Though the water seems not to move." Henceforward we know that Pound is going to be concerned with that which crumbles and that which does not. Sardinian corn-yield, ox-herds, ivory, gold, land are the usual material temptations straight out of Horace and of a tradition as old as Sappho: they also fit rather neatly into the frame of Poundian economic polemic and thus "mean" here more vividly than one might expect in a translation. Thus, the close attention he lavishes upon the first two Horatian stanzas; there is a startling warmth and luster in the presentation of these false desiderata, particularly in lines 6–7. The miss is so near: to possess land is only just to materialize the aesthetic act—the water seems not to move, then the land crumbles. Pound's next strophe, the material counter to "take note of flavors" of the earlier poem, falls into the old vehemence: "Ply pruning hook to the / Profit of some seller that he, the seller, / May drain Syra from gold out-size basins. . . ." The translation has got a bit wilder; "that the rich merchant may drain wine from gold cups, wine purchased by Syrian trade" is literally closer. The Latin poet is only mildly ironical (particularly as he is exploiting a character type common to contemporary love elegy) about the curious fact that the vintner labors for others' profit; Pound is still outraged.

So delicate is Horace's irony that he can modulate into a conventional celebration of the simple life ("me pascunt olivae") in midstanza, even midline without notable inconcinnity. Pound has climbed a rhetorical mountain and comes down hard—the poem breaks with the same effect as that of the curtal sonnet that precedes it. The shift in tone and attention comes almost with a shudder, but there is peaceful resolution with the submission of the old passion to the Horatian closure:

> Olives feed me, and endives and mallow roots.

With the qualification that if the vehemence was wrong, the values were right:

> Delight had I healthily in what lay handy provided.

And finally a more explicit turning to the consolations hinted in the last translation:

> Grant me now, Latoë:
>> Full wit in my cleanly age,
> Nor lyre lack me to tune the page.

Clarity of intellect in the moment of perception and creation. But "consolation" is precisely the wrong word. This poem turns away as if from a last temptation toward honesty and resolve, and that amounts to a kind of celebration.

Celebration is, of course, the central burden of C. 3.30, the last of Pound's translations of the fat and beery poet.

> Exegi monumentum aere perennius
> regalique situ pyramidum altius,
> quod non imber edax, non Aquilo impotens
> possit diruere aut innumerabilis
> annorum series et fuga temporum.
> non omnis moriar multaque pars mei
> vitabit Libitinam: usque ego postera
> crescam laude recens. dum Capitolium

scandet cum tacita virgine pontifex,
dicar, qua violens obstrepit Aufidus
et qua pauper aquae Daunus agrestium
regnavit populorum, ex humili potens
princeps Aeolium carmen ad Italos
deduxisse modos. sume superbiam
quaesitam meritis et mihi Delphica
Lauro cinge volens, Melpomene, comam.

The poem, the self-gratulatory epilogue to his first three books of Odes, is familiar enough to need no special introduction here. In its various aspects, the assertion of monumental achievement, the progress from modest beginnings to greatness, the defiance of time in the immortality of the poet through his verse, it has been quoted by any number of English poets. Pound too had long dallied with C. 3.30 in bits and pieces; there is the cheery mockery of "Monumentum Aere, Etc." (1917):

> In a few years no one will remember the *buffo,*
> No one will remember the trivial parts of me,
> The comic detail will be absent.
> As for you, you will rot in the earth.

And there is the rather ponderous revision of "Dum Capitolium Scandet":

> How many will come after me
> singing as well as I sing, none better;
> Telling the heart of their truth
>   as I have taught them to tell it;
> Fruit of my seed,
>   O my unnameable children.
> Know then that I loved you from afore-time,
> Clear speakers, naked in the sun, untrammelled.

And fragmentarily elsewhere.[10] Which may be evidence only that the thing hung in his mind. Why it did so may be unanswerable; we may have to settle for an understanding of *what* he finally did with it.

> This monument will outlast metal and I made it
> More durable than the king's seat, higher than pyramids.
> Gnaw of wind and rain?
>   Impotent
> The flow of years to break it, however many.

> Bits of me, many bits, will dodge all funeral,
> O Libitina-Persephone and, after that,
> Sprout new praise. As long as
> Pontifex and the quiet girl pace the Capitol

I shall be spoken where the wild flood Aufidus
Lashes, and Daunus ruled and parched farmland:

Power from lowliness: "First brought Aeolic song to Italian fashion"—
Wear pride, work's gain! O Muse Melpomene,
By your will bind the laurel.
　　　　　My hair, Delphic laurel.

There will from very few be any quibbling about whether this is or is not precisely a "translation," yet the tone, diction, and attitude of the first two lines will puzzle one for a moment. There is something outrageously simple about it; here is not the most literal but the plainest possible sense of the Latin. After the paternal intonations of "Dum Capitolium Scandet," this seems nearly the child's voice. And that is just the right voice. English readers have always looked askance at Horace's immodesty. But Pound captures the appealing innocence of the boast: "This monument will outlast metal and I made it. . . ." And that naive rhetoric of youth comes, crucially, hard upon "full wit in my cleanly age" and leads into

　　　Gnaw of wind and rain?
　　　　　　　　Impotent
The flow of years to break it, however many.

And we recall "gnaw" from C. 1.11:

　　　　　Winter is winter,
Gnawing the Tyrrhene cliffs with the sea's tooth.

And with it the complex of images it is part of and suggests by contrast, the zest of flavors, clarity, life's hunger for feeling. Nor do we forget that *that* is inextricably bound in C. 1.31 to the sound of the lyre and the tuning of the page. This last is then a full recapitulation of the dominant themes of the first two translations, and more. Impotent the flow of years to break Pound's monument, but the poem does, in a sense, break here:

Bits of me, many bits of me will dodge all funeral.

And the appeal of monumental imagery is shattered. What of poetry endures longer than metal or bronze is not the whole of constructed edifice, but the tightly knit pieces, the "entanglements" of words that manage coherence. Pound's line is light, tossed off, a kind of joke—and that is where he finds one of his deepest sympathies with Horace. For Horace's poem, too, embodies a joke, one whose point is sometimes altogether missed. C. 3.30 begins, "Exegi monumentum aere perennius . . ." in "stately" lesser Asclepiads. Monumental image succeeds image, "regalique situ pyramidum altius"; the immunity to time of these first three books is complete. Then comes the first turn—Horace will nearly always turn from the expected— "multaque pars mei vitabit Libitinam," and suddenly the poet is standing in for the poems and the organic unity of *that* figure won't suffice, only "multaque pars." The personified "corpus" is of course transitional, facing two ways and answering to two kinds of image. The second kind occupies the second half of the poem: "crescam laude recens . . . qua violens obstrepit Aufidus . . . princeps Aeolium carmen ad Italos deduxisse modos . . . lauro cinge . . . comam." Images of growth, movement, change, metamorphosis. Horace's poems may outlast bronze precisely because they are unlike it, apt to re-vision, reconstrual. "Dum capitolium / scandet cum tacita virgine pontifex" stipulates perhaps more than the perdurance of Rome, extending to the larger continuity of ceremonial human activity within the context of civil order. Some will remember Yeats here and won't be far wrong. The notion of the shifting frame of time, of context, is confirmed by the collage of verb tenses: "Where Aufidus roars . . . where Daunus, poor of water, ruled, I shall be spoken." This is the metamorphosis of Horace's own life, "ex humili potens," writ large. In spite of the long classical tradition of hearty boasting about poems (in Ennius, Propertius, Ovid, Martial, and the rest[11]), Horace is *playing* with the rhetoric of boast. He finally gives readers what they expect least, not a vaunt of monumental defiance to mutability, but an acknowledgment that continued engagement with posterity involves a kind of metamorphosis ("multaque pars mei"); revision and change, hence "growth" ("crescam laude recens"), is the essence of poetic life. And that amounts to an acknowledgment of the interdependency of writer and reader and of the evolving "geography" in which a poem is read. Configurations of Horace, interpretive and otherwise, to come depend critically on those whom, with Melpomene, he addresses: "et mihi Delphica / lauro cinge volens, Melpomene, comam."

Pound knew all this: his own metamorphosis of Libitina to Libitina-Persephone promising return and regermination, "to sprout new praise," is ample testimony. The essence of the poem is to make the old thing new: "First brought Aeolic song to Italian / Fashion." Usually a good reader, he knew that Horace's best poem about poetry was not the jumbled, contradictory *Ars Poetica,* but this ode. Although its indirection distances and generalizes, this work addresses what may be the writer's deepest concern, the relation of poem to history—the same ground the American poet covered in the translations of C. 1.11 and C. 1.31. "Take note of flavors" leads on a direct course to "Power from lowliness." Both refer to manners of mind, to the clarity of attention in the poem's moment of vivid life, and to humility in the knowledge that the poet's initial creative vision is not the single and final coherence. In this is a key recognition; it catches the tone of all the late recantations within and without the Cantos. But it is no confession of failure—not here: "Wear pride, work's gain!" And work *is* the gain:

O Muse Melpomene,
By your will bind the laurel.
My hair, Delphic laurel.

The laurel, the crown of posterity's attention to be bound and bound again, is also in apposition to "my hair," the natural crown of man and poet; and it is too the thing bound of words, written and read, just as this poem twines and turns them figurally on the page. And "Delphic" laurel, which is to say prophetic, turning forward, and so sharing the chief insight of Horace C. 3.30—learning from Horace. It is the old dependency of Horace and Pound and us. Remember, "I cannot make it cohere . . . I cannot make it flow through," but "it coheres all right." It flows through (one cannot avoid the old Poundian tag) the vortex, which is the momentary and perpetually reformative coherence of the Janus-facing *act* of the poem.

The three Horace translations of 1963 and 1964 form together as effective a "crown" to Pound's career, as conclusive a *sphragis*, as any he could devise. Better, indeed, than the piecemeal decline of the last Cantos. And it is significant, not just curious, that so fitting a closure comes through translation. It is not just that Pound thought best through the matrices of other languages, literatures, traditions. Rather, through resigning himself to their influences, he transfigured their impulses into startling new creation. For instance, in both the Propertius and the Horace there is some resignation of self, of dogmatism, so that in the former case it is the Propertian voice which offers the initial governance of diction, nuance, and tone. In the latter case, Horace dictates a kind of reorientation of the poet to his verse and the verse to the world. Horace, the master of technique, pressures Pound just as he does Bunting and any number of others. And Pound, of course, *would* respond in kind, technically, just as he has in these three translations. But the utter restraint of these pieces, the unwillingness to appropriate them, is, if not to let Horace speak definitively about Pound's art, to admit a profound and earlier unrecognized sympathy with the impulse of Horace's verse. In short, it amounts to a recognition that Horace was right all along; the art of poetry doesn't reside in "genius" or in the "granite acridity" of passion or in great themes (history, economics, usury) or in great subjects (Adams, Confucius, and the rest), but in the simple, enormously complex "tuning of the page," the song that passes and returns. It took fat, bald-headed Horace to teach Pound that or to remind him of what he said in 1912, that the poet should "suffer all drudgery to find some entanglement of words so subtle, so crafty, that they can be read without yawning after the reading of Pindar and Meleager" ("Osiris," 35).

On another level as well, sympathy with the kind of verse Pound discovered in Pindar, Meleager, and Horace may be deep indeed. There is a musical analogy of common currency. A prominent musicologist has recently revived the old characterization of Bach as an indifferent melodist, but consumate harmonist.[12] His linear melodic developments, rather than clear, unencumbered "lines," are often chords, broken into component parts or turned on their sides. Handel wrote melodies, "tunes"—however delicate and sophisticated. Poetry in some simplistic but telling way may be like that. Catullus, of the granite acridity, wrote melodies, Horace harmonies—each poetic element calling into play a number of others and not isolable from them. Which is a submission of passion to the volatile patterns of art.[13] Intricacies of meter, form, topos, convention, compounded by the always surprising turn from the expected, the slip from image to image not quite of the same order, all colored by the most delicate subtlety of thought, the wry smile. Pound didn't always write like that, but his best verse—that for which he'll be remembered long after people have tired of looking up the details of social credit or even some of the nicer things like Couvreur's Chou King—is found in his most textured, self-consciously inter-hering, entanglements of words: the Propertius, "Mauberley," the many and great nuggets within the Cantos. Which may be taken to suggest that Pound's achievement is not the striking innovation of the Cantos' open, agglutinative form,[14] nor even the ostensibly "fugal" structures of its decads, but rather what the Cantos, as the central document of Pound's poetic universe, contain: patternings of words, some brief, some extended, where languages, ideas, traditions, programs, forms, attain to singular, resonant harmonies. "Dances," just that, kinetic and formal inter-weavings, where "intellect" and "words" are indistinguishable, joined in motley symmetries.

*   *   *

This leads to something more general. The phenomenon of Ezra Pound translating poetry is a singular hallmark in twentieth-century letters. Its influence has been immense. Only a very few of those touched have been mentioned in these pages. It has established a climate much like that of an earlier age of great translations, the eighteenth century, but yet more experimental, more richly various in idea and accomplishment. Whigham's Catullus and Martial, Rexroth's Greek lyrics, Logue's Patroklea, Fitzgerald's Homer and *Aeneid*, Sisson's pieces from Catullus, Ovid, Vergil, and Horace—these and many more are things long to be read and pondered and worth the pondering. As we think of them in our desultory ways we must consider most critically the act of modern poets themselves considering ancient poems. That they do so is not a matter of service or of duty to the artifacts of a dessicated culture, an "old bitch gone in the teeth," but is a matter of discovering something *they* deem important. In its largest terms, the thing is as Macleod would have it, the poet trying to "enliven and enrich himself." That the poet's enrichment is the conduit to a larger cultural gain is obvious.

But less obvious may be the *kind* of enriching role translation has played in our time. On one level, it is plain that translation functions as a heuristic mode of perception. It is further of a character, while bound to particulars of time and place, that is still predominantly "textual"—as Pound seems to have discovered. Which is merely to say that the conventions of intercourse between poem and translation are not those of historical archaeology or comparative linguistics. They are more accurately the kinds of conventions that bind the Homeric epics to the *Aeneid* or the *Aeneid* to *Paradise Lost*. Not that the latter are examples of translation, but the *terms* of interaction, i.e., languages used in the frame of poetic composition, are the same. So much is true of all translations, even the feeblest crib. But within this grand rubric, twentieth-century translation (not all, but much of it), after Pound, has broken out of the timeworn channels of access and exchange. It asks questions never asked before. And in subtler ways, it sees the classics differently, brings them into dialogue under different terms. The same Catullus gives rise to the radically individual versions of Zukofsky, Whigham, and Sisson, and the question they together suggest is not, decidedly not, which of the three translations is "the best" or truest or even "most poetic." Rather they impel us to ask what each reveals to us about poetry then and now, which is to begin to explain how each in its way delights us.

Text (most literally) revising text. The analogy to contemporary modes of critical inspection is obvious. But it must be noted that Pound and other modern translators were there before the critics. Translations have become the means by which the poem re-poses itself—not just to a new age but other minds. And such reposition always involves reconstrual, reconfiguration. Pound gives us a Propertius whose facets turn light and color now here, now there, not at the expense of the laws of structure, semantics, syntax, or history (or even intent), but through all of these things as new coherences emerge at the nexus of poem and perceiving eye. This is not merely to speak of translations in terms dictated by what was once called "imitation." There have always been imitations of the sort Pope and Johnson made popular, and will be, but the underlying assumptions are different. Two centuries ago, texts were seen to hover in bilingual balance; what Johnson does in *London* is informed by, understood in juxtaposition with, Juvenal's Third. Johnson's poem was not meant as an avenue of critical approach as is Logue's Homer, say, or even the more subdued (in its particulars) Martial of Porter. Translation since Pound, whether one likes Pound or not, has come to signify a process of intellection, of turning a poem over and around, of discovery. The underlying assumption of *that*, as Horace well understood, is that mutability is at least one essential condition of literature. Which doesn't mean that poets don't care what Homer said or meant to say; quite the contrary, they would not spend the time with him if they didn't. But what Homer says does not always mean the same to all; he would not mean in 1918 what he did in 1914, to take the radical case. It is the literary sorting through of what and how he means for now and a moment from now that is the endlessly interesting and vitally important work of translation.

What of the classics, then? Have they been relegated by Pound's influence to a tiresome cycle of revision and re-vision? Have they become just another pre-text? That least of all. For the conviction, which Pound held passionately, that translating the classics enriches and instructs is founded in the assumption that the literatures of Rome and Greece matter, centrally, still; that they are worth the bother of thinking through. And that is some assurance that they will continue to be read—both ways. In a (now-) limited, but real sense, they are still the root and stem of our discourse, modernist and postmodern, and still offer patterns for our thought. That they can do so in such marvelous new configurations is just another feature of their wonder. And ours.

Notes

Introductory Essay

1. Preface to *Ovid's Epistles Translated by Several Hands*, quoted and discussed at some length by George Steiner, *After Babel: Aspects of Language and Translation* (London: Oxford University Press, 1975), 253–257. As famous as the passage is, it is not merely one of the usual bits on translation to be habitually trotted out to show that an author has read *something* on the subject. In Steiner's words, "Dryden's analysis remains memorable. . . . It laid down ideals and lines of discussion which are ours still" (253). That is not to say, however, that one ought blithely to accept Dryden's terms, "paraphrase," "metaphrase," and "imitation," or the tripartite structure of his thinking in this matter. Indeed, although in general there may be "kinds" of translation or catagories for which terms have been and will continue to be invented, it is well-nigh impossible to account for translation's multiplicity and full variety with such labels. A perusal of the theoretical literature makes that clear. It becomes even harder to exclude some efforts from the general rubric "translation" for their being too free or revisionary. One useful approach, then, may be to rely upon the most generous conception of the art (see note 25 below) and to focus critical attention on its particular manifestations, allowing theory to illuminate them when it will, but not insisting that they fit into its Procrustean beds.

2. Benjamin (Heidelberg, 1923), quoted from *Illuminations*, trans. Harry Zohn, ed. Hannah Arendt (New York: Harcourt, Brace and World, 1968), 73. The essay has been a surprisingly prominent influence in modern discussion.

3. David Stephen Ross, "Translation and Similarity," in *Translation Spectrum: Essays in Theory and Practice*, ed. Marilyn Gaddis Rose (Albany: SUNY Press, 1981), 8–22. See, too, the summary provided by Louis Kelly, *The True Interpreter: A History of Translation Theory and Practice in the West* (Oxford: Blackwell, 1979), 26–33.

4. See Marjorie Perloff's discussion of the question of aesthetic dominance in our century in terms of what she calls the expressionist and constructionist poles in "Pound/Stevens: whose era?" first published in *New Literary History* 13(Spring 1982): 485–514, and now conveniently found in her *The Dance of the Intellect* (Cambridge: Cambridge University Press, 1985), 1–32.

5. Knox offers us more than entertaining quips like this from *Let Dons Delight;* his two works on translation are worth a look: *The Trials of a Translator* (New York: Sheed and Ward, 1949) and *On English Translation* (Oxford: Clarendon Press, 1957).

6. Charterhouse and Exeter respectively. For more, see M. L. Clarke, *Classical Education in Britain, 1500–1900,* (London: Cambridge University Press, 1959).

7. A minor controversy has lately arisen concerning the integrity of some of Schliemann's procedures, the authenticity of some of his discoveries, and even his character. See W. Calder III, "Schliemann on Schliemann: A Study on the Use of Sources," *Greek, Roman, and Byzantine Studies* 13(1972): 335–53; W. G. Niederland, "An Analytic Inquiry in to the Life and Work of Heinrich Schliemann,"

in *Drives, Effects, Behavior,* ed. Max Schur (New York: International Universities Press, 1965), 2:369–96; David Traill, "Schliemann's Mendacity: Fire and Fever in California," *Classical Journal* 74(April–May 1979): 348–55; and Traill and Calder, eds., *Myth, Scandal, and History: The Heinrich Schliemann Controversy and a First Edition of The Mycenaean Diary* (Detroit: Wayne State University Press, 1985).

8. For a concise summary of classical studies in the nineteenth century, see Gilbert Highet's chapter "A Century of Scholarship" in *The Classical Tradition* (Oxford: Oxford University Press, 1949). Further discussion can of course be found in the old standard, J. E. Sandys, *A History of Classical Scholarship* (1908; reprint, Cambridge: Cambridge University Press, 1964), as well as in Rudolf Pfeiffer, *History of Classical Scholarship 1300–1850* (Oxford Clarendon Press, 1976) and U. von Wilamowitz-Moellendorff, *History of Classical Scholarship,* trans. Alan Harris, ed. Hugh Lloyd-Jones (London: Duckworth, 1982). See also Hugh Lloyd-Jones, *Blood for the Ghosts: Classical Influences in the Nineteenth and Twentieth Centuries* (London: Duckworth, 1982).

9. A "museum culture" is the suggestive term that Steiner has applied to this set of conditions wherein progressively more specialized and sophisticated knowledge and methodologies are exercised on ancient material removed from the currency of ordinary life—in Pound's words, "two gross of broken statues / . . . a few thousand battered books." See *In Bluebeard's Castle* (New Haven: Yale University Press, 1971).

10. From L. P. Hartley, *The Go-Between* (London: Hamish Hamilton, 1953).

11. This is one reason eighteenth-century "imitation" of the sort that asked its auditor to hold in mind the original while it worked its changes upon it has not much hope of application these days.

12. That is to say, as an aid to construal of the Greek or Latin or even as a text to discuss in English-only classrooms.

13. See *Instaurations* (Berkeley: University of California Press, 1979), 11–12 in particular, and his entire introduction in general.

14. "Alien" indeed, as one might judge from the prominence of classical myth and language in the literature of science fiction. See, for instance, C. Fredericks's discussion in, "Science Fiction and the World of Greek Myth," *Helios,* n. s., 2 (1975): 1–22.

15. Often eccentrically, as in Harold Bloom's study of Stevens, *The Poems of Our Climate* (Ithaca: Cornell University Press, 1976); see his usages of "ethos," "pathos," "logos," "aporia," "clinamen," and the rest.

16. See Donald S. Carne-Ross's (n. 13 above) fuller discussion, 15–16.

17. As has W. V. O. Quine, *Word and Object* (Cambridge: MIT Press, 1960).

18. "As did Augustine, Pound took translation to be essentially teaching, the central element in Herder's *Erklärung.* The various facets of the image run through his writings: he praises Laurence Binyon's Dante for 'shedding more light on Dante' than any other translation he had seen. This, too, is a point he makes of his own Cavalcanti: that any 'atrocities' in his translation are there to 'drive the reader's perception' far under the surface of the original. The translation is meant to come alive, to make the background of the original contemporary" (Kelly, *True Interpreter,* 53–54).

19. Donald Davie particularly takes exception to this. Answering Steiner's similar claim about the importance of Pound's experimental work with translation in the Propertius, Davie, in *Ezra Pound* (New York: Penguin, 1976), calls the assertion "dangerous": "Pound has indeed renovated the art of translation in our time, but this is not one of the works by which he did so!" (59). And, "the point is a crucial one, for *Homage to Sextus Propertius* is often presented as a model for translators to follow, it

deliberately and consistently incorporates mistranslation—" (58–59). It is, in part, the burden of my essays here to show, however one may lament it (and one may as well not lament it), that Pound's Propertius was decisive and influential as a model for subsequent translators. That influence, insofar as the poem is both novel and strikingly engaging as translation, will further be seen as far from execrable.

20. Derrida, most recently in *Difference in Translation*, ed. Joseph F. Graham (Ithaca: Cornell University Press, 1985), which includes essays by several hands as well as a previously unpublished essay by Derrida himself, "Des Tours de Babel." Barthes, Kristeva, Scholes, Cluysenaar play a rather prominent role in Susan Bassnett-McGuire's *Translation Studies* (London: Methuen, 1980). Davie has, of course, written extensively on Pound's translations in *Ezra Pound: Poet as Sculptor* (London: Routledge and Kegan Paul, 1965) and his later *Ezra Pound* (New York: Penguin, 1976) as well as generally, *Poetry in Translation* (Milton Keynes: The Open University Press, 1975). See also Terry Eagleton, "Translation and Transormation," *Stand* 19(1977): 72–77.

21. I notice that Ronnie Apter mentions this too in *Digging For Treasure: Translating after Pound* (New York: Peter Lang, 1984) as part of her discussion of the dissonace between Victorian and modern values and what Pound made of it in his translations. She quotes H. A. Mason: "The priggish-melancholy note of Aeneas, oh so conscious in his modesty of the nobility of the example he is setting his son, is exactly what the Victorians found 'edifying.' They are welcome to it" (142).

22. It may be arguable in fact that this mutability is the essential condition of *perception* in the reading of poetry, through which (and here the tools and methods of traditional scholarship come to bear) one may gain some nearer access to a more stable (because historically, generically localized) ground of "intended" meaning, its implicit privacy.

23. Eugene Nida and Charles Tabor, *The Theory and Practice of Translation* (Leiden: E. J. Brill, 1969). Nida's distinction between "dynamic equivalence" and "formal correspondence" has come to be frequently cited in translation studies. The first concept represents the "closest natural equivalent to the source language message" or the "quality of a translation in which the message of the original text has been so transported into the receptor language that the response of the receptor is essentially that of the original receptors. Frequently, much the form of the original text is changed. . . . (202)" "Formal correspondence" is much nearer to Benjamin's fidelity to the "original's mode of signification": the "quality of translation in which the features of the form of the source text have been mechanically reproduced in the receptor language (203)." As Nida has it, dynamic equivalence represents both meaning and the original "feel" (Pound's word) more clearly than the other.

24. "Editor's Introduction," *Comparative Criticism* 6 (1984): xix and xxv. See also Charles Tomlinson, *Poetry and Metamorphosis* (Cambridge: Cambridge University Press, 1983), Clark Lectures for 1982.

25. Steiner's "definition" of translation in *Poem into Poem* (Harmondsworth: Penguin, 1970), though too broad for some, is I think still the most useful: "I have taken translation to include the writing of a poem in which a poem in another language . . . is the vitalizing, shaping presence; a poem which can be read and responded to independently but which is not ontologically complete, a previous poem being its occasion and, in the literal sense, *raison d'être*" (34). Understood exactly, this is precise enough. It allows one to distinguish between what Vergil and Joyce do with Homer and what Pope or Robert Fitzgerald do. The first two examples utilize (not necessarily "imitate") elements of technique, convention, theme, character, even plot without reproducing or restating an original's artistic

purpose. If one may speak of intentions, there is a clear intent on the part of the later writer to construct a new artistic entity—using bits of the old that may show through here and there but in new configuration and purpose. Then again, "translation" may be construed broadly enough to encompass Pound's Propertius or Zukofsky's Catullus, for these are poems, whatever their accomplishment, that lack "ontological completeness" unless they are understood to be in some direct and correspondent relation to the poems that prompted them. It is important to note that the terms of the correspondence need not be conventional—literal in choice of word or identical in tone or style—but the relation must be central not only to the structure but to the identity of the translation. A translation will *compulsively* turn back, beginning, middle, and end, to its original. It may do much else, much that is anachronistic, but it will chiefly be a medium (however "distorting") between another, older work and us, the means by which another poem is called to mind.

Chapter 1. Pound's Propertius Again

1. *Ezra Pound: Poet as Sculptor;* see also J. J. Espey, "Towards Propertius," *Paideuma* 1 (Spring–Summer 1972): 63–74.

2. J. P. Sullivan's book, *Ezra Pound and Sextus Propertius: A Study in Creative Translation* (London: Faber and Faber, 1964) is still the essential study on this subject. All subsequent *Homage* scholarship, even that critical of Sullivan, has been indebted to him.

3. Sullivan's summary of the critical reception of and controversy around the work is quite good up until 1964, the date of his book's publication. In 1965 Jorge Luis Borges, "Note sur Ezra Pound, traducteur," *Les Cahiers de l'Herne,* nos. 6–7 (1965), also placed the translation in a literary-historical context and was appreciative, as was Thomas Drew-Bear, "Ezra Pound's 'Homage to Sextus Propertius,' " *American Literature* 37 (1965): 204–10. The old issue of Pound's competence with the Latin was raised again by G. M. Messing, "Pound's Propertius: The Homage and the Damage," in *Poetry and Poetics from Ancient Greece to the Renaissance: Studies in Honor of James Hutton,* ed. G. M. Kirkwood (Ithaca: Cornell University Press, 1975), 105–133, with more emphasis on the damage than the homage, although he appreciates the "poem" and finally comes to a view much like that of Davie. Mark Turner, "Propertius Through the Looking Glass: A Fragmentary Glance at the Construction of Pound's Homage," *Paideuma* 5 (Fall 1976): 241–65, is an interesting study of very general nature. Davie, in *Ezra Pound,* advances the theory that much of the Propertius is written in a kind of "babu English," a revision, although not a reversal, of his earlier opinions. Vincent Miller, "The Serious Wit of Pound's Homage to Sextus Propertius," *Contemporary Literature* 16 (Autumn 1975): 452–62, and Donald Monk, "How to Misread: Pound's Use of Translation," in *Ezra Pound: The London Years: 1908–1920,* ed. Philip Grover (New York: AMS, 1976), 61–88, both follow Davie's (I believe) mistaken lead. One may find a literary analysis not unrelated to the sort Harold Bloom practices in Ron Thomas's chapter on the Propertius in *The Latin Masks of Ezra Pound* (Ann Arbor: UMI Research Press, 1983), 39–58.

Perhaps here is the place to note a very few of the more important works on the classical side from which I have generally drawn in this chapter: A. W. Allen, " 'Sincerity' and the Roman Elegists," *Classical Philology* 45 (1950): 145–60; J.-P. Boucher, *Etudes sur Properce: Problèmes d'inspiration et d'art* (Paris: E. de Boccard, 1965); H. E. Butler and E. A. Barber, *The Elegies of Propertius* (Oxford: Clarendon Press, 1933); W. A. Camps, *Propertius Elegies: Book 1* (Cambridge: Cambridge University Press, 1961), Book 2 (1967), Book 3 (1966), Book 4 (1965). W. Clausen,

"Callimachus and Roman Poetry," *Greek, Roman, and Byzantine Studies* 5(1965): 181–96; Margaret Hubbard, *Propertius* (London: Duckworth, 1974); G. Luck, *The Latin Love Elegy* (London: Methuen, 1969); R. Lucot, "Problèmes de creation chez Properce," *Pallas* 10(1961): 59–68; J. K. Newman, *Augustus and the New Poetry* (Brussels: *Latomus*, 1967); D. R. Shackleton Bailey, *Propertiana* (Cambridge: Cambridge University Press, 1956); F. Solmsen, "Propertius and Horace," *Classical Philology* 43 (1948): 105–9; J. P. Sullivan, *Propertius: A Critical Introduction* (Cambridge: Cambridge University Press, 1976); H. Trankle, *Die Sprachkunst des Properz und die Tradition der lateinischen Dichtersprache, Hermes Einzelschriften,* Heft 15 (Wiesbaden: Steiner, 1960); W. Wimmel, *Kallimachos in Rom: Die Nachfolge seines apologetischen Dichtens in der Augusteerzeit, Hermes Einzelschrift,* Heft 16 (Wiesbaden: Steiner, 1960). See my bibliography for more.

4. *The London Magazine* 3(April 1963): 49—a comment not directed at the Propertius alone but nonetheless a controversial attack that has generated its own little industry of response and reaction.

5. Both Kelly in his admirable historical study of translation theory, *The True Interpreter,* and Steiner in his equally ambitious *After Babel* provide exhaustive bibliographies to which I refer the reader. See also Kelly's more recent general bibliography in *Comparative Criticism* 6 (1984): 347–59.

6. Knox, *On English Translation,* 4, cited by Steiner, *After Babel,* 239.

7. For the "sacramental" quality, see Kelly's discussion, *True Interpreter,* 54–55 and passim.

8. William Gardner Hale, "Pegasus Impounded," *Poetry* 14(April 1919): 52–55, was the first of many condescending detractors. The famous *New Age* review, 26(1919): 62, was witty and perceptive; for all its scathing irony, it comes close to admiring the poem.

9. See Sullivan's review of the early negative comment, *Ezra Pound and Sextus Propertius* 3–16.

10. Cicero, *Libellus de optimo genere oratorum;* Horace, *Ars Poetica;* Augustine, *De magistro,* and *De doctrina christiana;* Boethius, preface to his translation of the *Isogoge* of Porphyry.

11. Cited and discussed by Kelly, *True Interpreter,* 44.

12. The relevance of these "personae" is raised and developed by many: Sullivan, *Ezra Pound and Sextus Properties,* 25–31; G. T. Wright, *The Poet in the Poem* (Berkeley: University of California, 1960), 124–57; Thomas, in a different way, *Latin Masks of Ezra Pound,* passim.

13. *The Journal and Letters of Stephen Mackenna,* ed. E. R. Dodds (London: Constable and Co., 1936), 114. See Steiner's discussion of Mackenna, *After Babel,* 267–69.

14. Sanford Schwartz, *The Matrix of Modernism: Pound, Eliot, and Early Twentieth-Century Thought* (Princeton: Princeton University Press, 1985), 147. Schwartz's chapter on Pound describes the poet's hostile reaction to the "threat of coercive uniformity in virtually every sphere of human endeavor" (115) and his compensating search of the past to bring lost forms of expression, precisely as new expressive potential, into modern currency. Both tendencies are clearly in evidence in the *Homage.*

15. G. M. Messing, (see n. 3) 118; his article, although I disagree with its conclusions is the best of the skeptical treatments of Pound's Latin skills.

16. For another answer, see Thomas's survey of Pound's Latin experience in the appendix to his *Latin Masks of Ezra Pound.*

17. See Introduction, note 17.

18. The language of Steiner in his *After Babel*. Steiner's four-stage "process" of translation is at the center of his contribution to translation theory. To begin, "trust": an "investment of belief" that there is something there worth translating. Then, "aggression": an act of aggressive interpretation inherently violent—"one breaks a code." This stage derives some of its tenor from Quintilian's "certamen," but rather than rivalry, indicates the necessary intellectual appropriation when one "comprehends" another. Third, "incorporation": placement of the new poem in the native language, whether with full idiomatic "at-homeness" or perhaps with some more marginal texture or degree of assimilation—Steiner instances Nabokov's *Onegin*. Finally, "restitution": an attempted compensation for the necessary damage a translation does (see 296–303).

19. Hale "Pegasus Impounded," 52, Messing, *"Pound's Propertius,"* 129, respectively.

20. See note 18.

21. See Frank Kermode's discussion in *The Classic: Literary Images of Permanence and Change* (New York: Viking, 1975), 134 and passim.

22. Wright's convincing argument deserves to be read in its full context. See note 12 above.

23. A discussion of the plausibility of such a view of the Roman poet can be found in Sullivan, "Leptotes and logopoeia" in *Propertius: A Critical Introduction*, 147–58.

Chapter 2. Memory's Tropes

1. Among those who have: Richard Emil Braun, "The Original Language: Some Postwar Translations of Catullus," *Grosseteste Review* 3(Winter 1970): 28–34; Alan Brownjohn, "Caesar 'ad Some," *New Statesman*, 1 August 1969, 151; Robert Conquest, "An Abomination of Moab," *Encounter* 34(May 1970): 56–63; Guy Davenport, "Louis Zukofsky," *Agenda* 8(Autumn–Winter 1970): 130–37; David M. Gordon, "Three Notes on Zukofsky's *Catullus* I 'Catullus viii': 1939–1960" in *Louis Zukofsky: Man and Poet*, ed. Carroll F. Terrell (Orono, Maine: National Poetry Foundation, 1979), 371–81; Burton Hatlen, "Catullus Metamorphosed," *Paideuma* 7(Winter 1978): 539–45, later expanded as "Zukofsky as Translator" in *Louis Zukofsky: Man and Poet*, 345–64; Kelly, *The True Interpreter;* André Lefèvre, *Translating Poetry: Seven Strategies and a Blueprint* (Assen/Amsterdam: Jan Gorcum, 1975); Burton Raffel, "No Tidbit Love You Outdoors Far as a Bier: Zukofsky's Catullus," *Arion* 8(Autumn 1969): 435–45.

This is obviously not the place for a general bibliography on Catullus, but a few works that have been a help are the commentaries by Wilhelm Kroll, *Catull* (1923; reprint, Stuttgart: Teubner, 1959 and 1968. and C. J. Fordyce, *Catullus* (1961; reprint, Oxford: Clarendon Press, 1965 and 1978) and a range of studies including: Eric A. Havelock, *The Lyric Genius of Catullus* (Oxford: Oxford University Press, 1939); Jean Granarolo, *L'Oevre de Catulle. Aspects Religieux, Ethiques et Stylistiques* (Paris: les Belles lettres, 1967); A. E. Wheeler, *Catullus and the Traditions of Ancient Poetry* (Berkeley: University of California Press, 1934); K. Quinn, *The Catullan Revolution* (Cambridge: Cambridge University Press, 1959); T. P. Wiseman, *Catullan Questions* (Leicester: Leicester University Press, 1969); E. Shafer, *Das Verhältnis von Erlebnis und Kunstgestalt bei Catull, Hermes Einzelschriften*, Heft 18 (Wiesbaden: Steiner, 1966), D. O. Ross, *Style and Tradition in Catullus* (Cambridge: Harvard University Press, 1970).

2. These are among the more dramatic of the reproofs; Hatlen cites them, and more, in his "Zukofsky as Translator" mentioned in note 1.

3. I use the singular here and afterwards for convenience and because Celia

Zukofsky has given full credit for the *poetry* to her husband—although the value of her collaboration, especially her work with the Latin, can be by no means discounted. See Hatlen, "Catullus Metamorphosed," 539.

4. It has been pointed out correctly that "phonetic" and "phonemic" do not at all suggest the same thing. In describing Zukofsky's work in the following passage, since I am paraphrasing him, I follow Lefèvre's use of "phonemic."

5. See K. K. Ruthven's *A Guide to Ezra Pound's Personae (1926)* (Berkeley: University of California Press, 1969), 213, for a fuller selection.

6. It is true, as a reader has commented, that Pound is translating from an earlier to a later stage of the same language and hence may depend upon a linguistic "memory" more vivid than Zukofsky's with his Latin. That may not have prevented the poet from imitating Pound's technique, however, Latin being "at home" in English more than most of us are aware.

7. Lots of discussion on poem 11 either by itself or in its relation to 51; see for instance Steele Commager, "Notes on Some Poems of Catullus," *Harvard Studies in Classical Philology* 70(1965): 82–110; I. Balogh, "Catulls Scheltelied auf Lesbia," *Philologus* 85(1929): 103–5; F. A. Todd, "Catullus 11," *The Classical Review* 55(1941): 70–73; T. E. Kinsey, "Catullus 11," *Latomus* 24(1965): 537–44, as well as comments in Fordyce and Kroll.

Henceforward in this chapter, in order to distinguish between Latin and English (untitled) poems, I shall employ roman and arabic poem numbers respectively—and leave off doing so when that ceases to serve a useful purpose, as roman numbers are cumbersome things.

8. See also Hatlen's discussion in "Zukofsky as Translator."

9. Something my own ear was too dull to notice; Peter Firchow's was not.

10. Richard Braun, in "The Original Language," makes the point that Zukofsky's translation is for Latinists who "can be forced to discover more English" (31) by attending to what Zukofsky makes of the Latin. I think this may not be precisely right, as my discussion makes clear, but it represents a valuable insight about the importance of the Latin the general spirit of which I second.

11. The literature on this particular stanza and on poem LI in general is very extensive. The commentaries and Commager's article (cited above, note 7) are good places to begin. For more: Bruno Snell, "Sappho c. 2," *Hermes* 66(1931): 71–90; W. Ferrari, "Il c. 51 di Catullo," *Annali della Scuola Normale Superiore di Pisa* 2, 7(1938): 59ff.; R. Lattimore, "Sappho 2 and Catullus 51," *Classical Philology* 39(1944); 184–87; L. Ferrero, *Interpretazione di Catullo* (Turin: Rosenberg and Sellier, 1955); E. A. Fredericksmeyer, "On the Unity of Catullus 51," *Transactions and Proceedings of the American Philological Association* 106(1965): 153–63; H. A. Khan, "Color Romanus in Catullus 51," *Latomus* 25 (1966): 448–60; A. J. Woodman, "Some Implications of Otium in Cat. 51, 13–16," *Latomus* 25(1966): 217–66.

Chapter 3. "And Wit Its Soul"

1. See Eliot's preface to his edition of Ezra Pound's *Selected Poems* (London: Faber and Faber, 1949), 12; see, as well, Peter Schneeman's unpublished dissertation, "Ezra Pound and the Act of Translation" (University of Minnesota, 1972), which takes note of Eliot's attitude in its substantial discussion, in one chapter, of Pound's translations and imitations of classical epigrams.

2. For a quick and reasonably accurate discussion of the classical epigram—upon which I've drawn—see Peter Jay's introductory essay to his *The Greek Anthology* (New York: Oxford University Press, 1973). One will find more in C. M. Bowra, *Greek Lyric Poetry from Alcman to Simonides* (Oxford: Oxford University Press,

1961). Of course one should look at the several volumes of texts and commentaries prepared by A. S. F. Gow and D. L. Page for Cambridge University Press of Greek epigrams, *inter alia,* to be found in the Greek Anthology. For a selection of English versions of the epigram and some sense of its English history, see Geoffrey Grigson's anthology, *The Faber Book of Epigrams and Epitaphs* (London: Faber and Faber, 1977).

Useful general works on Martial and his epigrams are surprisingly few; J. P. Sullivan's new study—at this moment in press—(Cambridge: Cambridge University Press, 1987) will be a welcome addition. Among others: A. G. Carrington, *Aspects of Martial's Epigrams* (Eton: Shakespeare Head Press, 1960); J. W. Duff, "Varied Strains in Martial," in *Classical and Mediaeval Studies in Honor of E. K. Rand* edited by Leslie Weber Jones (Freeport: Books for Libraries Press, 1968), 87–99; Peter Howell in his commentary on Book I of The Epigrams (London: Athlone, 1980); C. W. Mendell, "Martial and the Satiric Epigram," *Classical Philology* 17(1922): 1–20; L. Pepe, *Marziale* (Napoli, 1950); U. Scamuzzi, "Contributo ad una obiettiva conoscenza della vita e dell' opera di Marco Valerio Marziale," *Revista di Studi Classici* 14(1966): 149–207; O. Seel, "Ansatz zu einer Martial-Interpretation," *Antike und Abendland* 10(1961): 53–76; E. Siedschlag, *Zur Form von Martials Epigrammen* (Berlin: Mielke, 1977); K. F. Smith, *Martial the Epigrammatist and Other Essays* (Baltimore: Johns Hopkins University Press, 1920).

3. Ruthven makes the point in *Guide To Ezra Pound's Personae,* 82.

4. J. W. Mackail, quoted by T. K. Whipple in *Martial and the English Epigram from Sir Thomas Wyatt to Ben Jonson,* University of California Publications in Modern Philology, vol. 10, no. 4 (Berkeley 1925), 281.

5. Lacking a more up to date history of the earlier epigram in English, one should turn to Whipple for a brief but good survey of these poets' work in the genre.

6. See J. P. Sullivan, "Martial's Sexual Attitudes," *Philologus* 123 (1979): 288–312.

7. Eight in fact. Cunningham's poetry is quoted from *The Collected Poems and Epigrams of J. V. Cunningham* (London: Faber and Faber, 1971).

8. See Grigson, *Epigrams and Epitaphs,* 254.

9. See Kelly, *True Interpreter,* 68–99; Kelly invokes Buhler as an answer in part to Postgate: "It is unfortunate that usage has not provided distinctive names for translation which primarily regards the author, and translation which primarily regards the reader" (Kelly, *True Interpreter,* 243).

10. I should mention that Kelly uses his terms as a means to discuss, more subtly than we are able to do otherwise, the purposes and objectives of certain discernible "kinds" of translation. I am borrowing them, provisionally, as a means of getting at distinct qualities and perhaps intentions within translations that point to a more generally applicable (as I think it) interdependence between poem and version.

11. Gerard Genette, *Figures II* (Paris: Seuil, 1969), 150, cited in Jonathan Culler, *Structuralist Poetics* (Ithaca Cornell University, 1975), 164.

12. I acknowledge here a debt to D. R. Smith's dissertation-in-progress, "Programmatic Images in Latin Satire," University of Minnesota.

13. See Keith Preston's article, "Martial and Formal Literary Criticism," *Classical Philology* 15 (October 1920): 351.

14. See Sullivan, "Martial's Sexual Attitudes," cited in 6 above.

Chapter 4. Disjecti Membra Poetae?

1. The importance of understanding the scarcity of our knowledge of Sappho's lyric fragments, and the role that plays in our reading of them, is nicely set out by

W. R. Johnson in *The Idea of Lyric: Lyric Modes in Ancient and Modern Poetry* (Berkeley: University of California Press, 1982), 24–26.

2. For a fairly recent treatment of Horatian influences in the eighteenth century, one might look to R. M. Ogilvie's *Latin and Greek: A History of the Influence of the Classics on English Life from 1600–1918* (London: Routledge and Kegan Paul, 1964), 34–73. See, too, Caroline Goad, *Horace and the English Literature of the Eighteenth Century* (New Haven: Yale University Press, 1918).

3. Although R. G. M. Nisbett and Margaret Hubbard, the latest commentators on Horace's Odes 1 and 2, in *A Commentary on Horace: Odes* (Oxford: Clarendon Press, 1970), have it as their "third."

The commentaries of Nisbett and Hubbard are of course a good place to start in looking for a fairly recent critical view of the poet. Niall Rudd has lately written two good general essays on Horace, "A Critique of the Traditional Stereotype" and "A Critique of the Academic Dichotomy" in the *Cambridge History of Classical Literature* vol. 2, Latin Literature, ed. E. J. Kenney and Wendell Clausen (Cambridge: Cambridge University Press, 1982). A few other discussions of the poet, particularly with respect to the odes, are N. E. Collinge, *The Structure of Horace's Odes* (London: Oxford University Press, 1961); Steele Commager, *The Odes of Horace: A Critical Study* (New Haven: Yale University Press, 1962); the essays by Margaret Hubbard, David West, and Valerie Edden in C. D. N. Costa, ed., *Horace* (London: Routledge and Kegan Paul, 1973); E. Fraenkel, *Horace* (Oxford: Oxford University Press, 1957); the essays by W. R. Johnson, as foreword and afterword to Burton Raffel's quite fine translation, *The Essential Horace* (San Francisco: North Point Press, 1983); the commentary of A. Kiessling and R. Heinze, *Horaz I, Oden und Epoden* (Berlin: Weidmann, 1958); J. Marouzean, "Horace, assembleur de mots," *Emerita* 4(1936): 365–74; G. Pasquali, *Orazio Lirico* (Florence: Le Monnier, 1920, 1964); V. Pöschl, "Horaz," *Fondation Hardt: Entretiens sur L'Antiquité Classique*, 2 (Geneva: Vandocuures, 1956), 93–115; K. Reckford, *Horace* (New York: Twayne, 1969); L. P. Wilkinson, *Golden Latin Artistry* (Cambridge: Cambridge University Press, 1963) and *Horace and His Lyric Poetry* (Cambridge: Cambridge University Press, 1945, 1951).

4. *Werke,* Taschenausgabe (Leipsig: E. Wiegandt, 1906), 10:343. Quoted by Commager and others.

5. The review, "Horacescope," of two translations by, respectively, Charles E. Passage and Burton Raffel will be found in *The New York Review of Books* 10 May 1984, 7–8, and the volume of *Arion* referred to is 9 (Summer–Autumn 1970).

6. Quoted by Sister Victoria Marie Forde, "The Translations and Adaptations of Basil Bunting," in *Basil Bunting: Man and Poet,* ed. Carroll F. Terrell (Orono: National Poetry Foundation, 1980), 311.

7. See the comments on this by Nisbett and Hubbard, *Commentary on Horace,* 170.

8. *Arion* (Summer–Autumn 1970) reprints Pound's essay from *Criterion* 9(1929–30): 217–27.

9. Thomas has commented extensively on this essay in his final chapter, "Horace as Demimask," from *Latin Masks of Ezra Pound,* 117–39. Thomas traces Pound's attitude to Horace from his earliest comments within and without the poetry through the final three Horace translations to show a pattern of rejection and acceptances of the Roman poet leading to a late "returning sympathy." The whole of his analysis, as valuable and informative as it is, is couched in terms of literary psychoanalysis, thus naturally arriving at conclusions about the poet's states of mind in his "lifelong quest for selfhood" rather than about states of poetry. The former strikes me as nearly always conjectural, the latter a good deal less so. Particularly

open to debate may be Thomas's conclusion that Pound's late reconciliation with Horace as psychological persona involves a "settling" for Horace, as "demimask," after his having failed to earn the full epic mask of Vergil.

10. See Thomas's summary, *Latin Masks of Ezra Pound*, 124–39.

11. Ennius: see Cicero, *Tusculan Disputations*, 1.34; Propertius: 4.1.59–66; Ovid: *Amores* 1.15.41–42. and *Metamorphoses* 15. 871–79; Martial: 8.3.5–8, among others.

12. Christopher Hogwood in a recent National Public Radio interview.

13. This is of course related to but not identical with Pound's description of the structure of the Cantos as resembling a fugue: "theme, response, countersujet. . . ." See Kay Davis's discussion in her *Fugue and Fresco: Structure in Pound's Cantos* (Orono: National Poetry Foundation, 1984), 71–94.

14. See Marjorie Perloff's discussion of analyses by Rosenthal and Hesse in *The Dance of The Intellect* (Cambridge: Cambridge University Press, 1985), 11.

Select Bibliography

The following is a selective compilation of articles and books of general interest; fuller bibliographies of translation theory and like information can be found in Steiner (*After Babel*) Kelly (*The True Interpreter* and his list in *Comparative Literature* 6), Bassnett-McGuire, and the journals *Babel* (Akademiae Kiado, Budapest), *Meta* (University of Montreal), the *Yearbook of Comparative and General Literature* (Indiana University, Bloomington), and the Texas (and Boston) journals *Arion* and *Delos*.

Adams, Robert M. 1930. *Proteus: His Lies, His Truth: Discussions of Literary Translation*. New York: Norton.

Aldington, Richard, trans. 1919. *Greek Songs in the Manner of Anachreon*. Poets translation series, 2nd set, no. 1, London: Egoist.

Alexander, Michael. 1979. *The Poetic Achievement of Ezra Pound*. Berkeley: University of California Press.

Alvarez, A. 1956. Ezra Pound: The Qualities and Limitations of Translation-Poetry." *Essays in Criticism* 6(April): 171–89.

Amos, Flora Ross. 1920. *"Early Theories of Translation."* Ph.D. diss., Columbia University.

Apter, Ronnie. 1984. *Digging for the Treasure: Translation after Pound*. New York: Peter Lang.

Arnold, Matthew. 1880. "On Translating Homer." In *Essays in Criticism*. New York: MacMillan, 284–424.

Arrowsmith, Wm. and R. Shattuck, eds. *The Craft and Context of Translation: A Symposium*. Austin: University of Texas Press for the Humanities Research Center.

Austin, R. G. 1956. *Some English Translations of Vergil*. Liverpool: Liverpool University Press.

Bagg, Robert. 1969. "Translating the Abyss: On Robert Fitzgerald's *Odyssey.*" *Arion* 8 (Spring): 51–65.

Balogh, I. 1929. "Catulls Scheltelied auf Lesbia." *Philologus* 85 : 103–5.

Barnard, Mary. 1978. "A Communication on Greek Metric, Ezra Pound, and Sappho." *Agenda* 16 : 62–68.

———. 1984. *Assault on Mount Helicon*. Berkeley: University of California Press.

Bassnett-McGuire, Susan. 1980. *Translation Studies*. London: Methuen.

Bate, W. Jackson. 1970. *The Burden of the Past and the English Poet*. Cambridge, Mass.: Belknap Press.

Bates, E. S. 1936. *Modern Translation*. London: Oxford University Press.

Beaugrande, Robert de. 1978 *Factors in a Theory of Poetic Translation*. Amsterdam and Assen: Van Gorcum.

Beede, Grace Lucille. 1936. Vergil and Aratus: A Study in the Art of Translation. Ph.D. diss., University of Chicago.

Belloc, Hilaire. 1931. *On translation.* (Taylorian Lecture, 1931.) Oxford: Clarendon Press.

Benjamin, Walter. 1969. "Die Aufgabe des Übersetzers" in *Das Problem des Übersetzens* edited by H. J. Störig. Stutgart: Govert, 182–95.

Boucher, J.-P. 1965. *Etudes sur Properce: Problèmes d'inspiration et d'art.* Paris: E. de Boccard.

Bovie, Palmer. 1975. "Complete Translations." *MLN* 90:800–808.

Bowra, C. Maurice. 1961. *Greek Lyric Poetry from Alcman to Simonides.* Oxford: Oxford University Press.

Braun, Richard. 1975. "Translation: The Problem of Purpose." *MLN* 90:784–99.

Bridges, Robert. 1916. *Ibant Obscuri: An Experiment in the Classical Hexameter.* Oxford: Clarendon Press.

Brink, C. O. 1971. *Horace on Poetry: The Ars Poetica.* Cambridge: Cambridge University Press.

Brower, Reuben A., ed. 1959. *On Translation.* Harvard Studies in Comparative Literature, 73. Cambridge: Harvard University Press.

———. 1974. *Mirror on Mirror. Translation, Imitation, Parody.* Cambridge: Harvard University Press.

Browning, Robert. 1873. *The Agamemnon.* London. See, also, collected editions of Browning.

Brownjohn, Alan. 1969. "Caesar 'ad Some." *New Statesmen,* 1 August, 151.

Bunting, Basil. 1936. Review of E. S. Bate's *Modern Translation* in *Criterion* 15 (July): 714–16.

———. *Collected Poems.* 1978. Oxford: Oxford University Press. This edition is cited parenthetically in the text as *CP.*

Butler, H. E., and E. A. Barber. 1933. *The Elegies of Propertius.* Oxford: Clarendon Press.

Butler, Samuel. 1898. *The Iliad.* London and New York: Longmans.

Cairns, Francis. 1972. *Generic Composition in Greek and Latin Poetry.* Edinburgh: Edinburgh University Press.

Campbell, George. 1789. *The Four Gospels.* London.

Camps, W. A. 1961, 1967, 1966, 1975. *Propertius Elegies,* bks. 1–4. Cambridge: Cambridge University Press.

Carne-Ross, D. S. 1979. *Instaurations.* Berkeley: University of California Press.

Carrington, A. G. 1960. *Aspects of Martial's Epigrams.* Eton: Shakespeare Head Press.

Catford, J. C. 1965. *A Linguistic Theory of Translation: An Essay in Applied Linguistics.* Language and Learning, 8. London: Oxford University Press.

Catullus. 1958. *C. Valerii Catulli Carmina.* Edited by R.A.B. Mynors. Oxford: Clarendon Press.

Catullus. 1892. *Catulli Tibulli Properti Carmina.* Edited by L. Mueller. Leipsig: Teubner.

Chukovsky, Korne: Ivanovich. 1984. *The Art of Translation.* Edited and translated by Lanoun G. Leighton. Knoxville: University of Tennessee Press.

Clarke, M. L. 1959. *Classical Education in Britain, 1500–1900*. London and Cambridge: Cambridge University Press.

Cohen, John M. 1962. *English Translators and Translations*. London: published for the British Council by Longmans.

Collinge, N. E. 1961. *The Structure of Horace's Odes*. London: Oxford University Press.

Commager, Steele. 1962. *The Odes of Horace: A Critical Study*. New Haven, Yale University Press.

———. 1965. "Notes on Some Poems of Catullus." *Harvard Studies in Classical Philology* 70 : 82–110.

Conley, Carey H. 1927. *The First English Translators of the Classics*. New Haven: Yale University Press; London: Oxford University Press.

Conquest, Robert. 1970. "An Abomination of Moab." *Encounter* 34 (May): 56–63.

Corman, Cid. 1980. "Earwork." In *Basil Bunting: Man and Poet*, edited by Carroll F. Terrell 293–299. Orono: National Poetry Foundation.

Costa, C. D. N., ed. 1973. *Horace*. London: Routledge and Kegan Paul.

Cunningham, J. V. 1971. *Collected Poems and Epigrams*. London: Faber and Faber. This edition is cited parenthetically in the text as *CP*.

Davenport, Guy. 1970. "Louis Zukofsky." *Agenda* 8 (Autumn–Winter): 130–37.

Davie, Donald. 1967. "The Translatability of Poetry." *The Listener* 78 : 838–40.

———. 1975. *Poetry in Translation*. Milton Keynes: The Open University Press.

———. 1965. *Ezra Pound. Poet as Sculptor*. London: Routledge and Kegan Paul.

———. 1976. *Ezra Pound*. New York: Penguin.

Day Lewis, C. 1963. "On Translating Poetry." In *Essays by Divers Hands;* n.s. 32. Wedmere Memorial Lecture, 1962. London: Oxford University Press, 18–36.

Dillon, Wentworth [Roscommon]. 1971. *An Essay on Translated Verse 1685*. Facsimile edition, Menston: Scolar Press.

Duckett, Eleanor S. 1925. *Catullus in English Poetry*. Smith College Classical Studies, 6. Northampton, Mass.

Eagleton, Terry. 1977. "Translation and Transformation." *Stand* 19 : 72–77.

Espey, J. J. 1972. "Towards Propertius." *Paideuma* 1(Spring–Summer): 63–74.

Firth, J. R. 1970. *The Tongues of Men and Speech*. London: Oxford University Press.

Forde, Sister Victoria Marie, S.C. 1980. "The Translations and Adaptations of Basil Bunting." In *Basil Bunting: Man and Poet*, edited by, Carroll F. Terrell, 301–42. Orono: National Poetry Foundation.

Fordyce, C. J. [1961] 1965, 1978. *Catullus*. Oxford: Clarendon Press.

Fraenkel, Eduard. 1963. *Early Greek Poetry and Philosophy*. Translated by Moses Hadas and J. Willis. Oxford: Clarendon Press.

———. *Horace*. 1957. Oxford: Oxford University Press.

Frost, W. 1955. *Dryden and the Art of Translation*. New Haven: Yale University Press.

Gildersleeve, B. L. 1975. "*Risus ab angulo:* A BLG Chrestomathy." Edited by Richard Macksey. *MLN* 90 : 940–71.

Goad, Caroline. 1918. *Horace and the English Literature of the Eighteenth Century*. New Haven: Yale University Press.

Goethe, Wolfgang von. 1956. *Dichtung und Wahrheit. In Vermishte Schriften*, edited by S. Scheibe, 361–405. Berlin: Tempel-Verlag.

Graham, Joseph F., ed. 1985. *Difference in Translation*. Ithaca: Cornell University Press.

Granarolo, Jean. 1967. *L'Oevre de Catulle. Aspects Religieux, Ethiques, et Stylistiques*. Paris: les Belles lettres.

Graves, Robert. 1955. *The Crowning Privilege*. London: Cassell and Co.

———. 1965. "Moral Principles in Translation." *Encounter* 24 : (April) 47–55.

Greene, Thomas. 1982. *The Light in Troy: Imitation and Discovery in Renaissance Poetry*. New Haven: Yale University Press.

Grierson, Herbert. 1948. *Verse Translation*. Oxford: Oxford University Press.

Grigson, Geoffrey, ed. 1977. *The Faber Book of Epigrams and Epitaphs*. London: Faber and Faber.

Guenthner, F. and Guenthner-Reutter, M., eds. 1978. *Meaning and Translation. Philosophical and Linguistic Approaches*. London: Duckworth.

Guttinger, Fritz. 1963. *Zielsprache: Theorie und Technik des Uebersetzens*. Zurich: Manesse.

Hale, William Gardner. 1919. "Pegasus Impounded." *Poetry* 14(April): 52–55.

Harrington, L. P. 1923. *Catullus and His Influence. Our Debt to Greece and Rome*. New York: Cooper Square.

Havelock, Eric A. 1939. *The Lyric Genius of Catullus*. Oxford: Oxford University Press.

Hays, James A. 1975. "The Translator and the Form-Content Dilemma." *MLN* 90 : 838–48.

Highet, Gilbert. 1961. "Beer Bottle on the Pediment." *Horizon* 3(January): 116–18.

———. 1949. *The Classical Tradition*. New York and London: Oxford University Press.

Holmes, James S. 1970. *The Nature of Translation*. International Conference on Translation as an Art, Bratislava, 1968. Mouton: Publishing House of the Slovak Academy of Sciences.

Horace. 1901. *Q. Horati Flacci Opera*. Edited by E. Wickham. Oxford: Clarendon Press.

Housman, A. E. 1899. Review of *On the Use of Classical Meters in English* by W. J. Stone, *Classical Review* 13 : 317–19.

Hubbard, Margaret. 1974. *Propertius*. London: Duckworth.

Jacobs, Carol. 1975. "The Monstrosity of Translation." *MLN* 90 : 755–66.

Jacobsen, Eric. 1958. *Translation: A Traditional Craft*. Copenhagen: Gyldenalske Boghandel.

Jay, Peter, ed. and trans. 1973. *The Greek Anthology*. New York: Oxford University Press.

Jenkyns, Richard. 1982. *Three Classical Poets: Sappho, Catullus, Juvenal*. London: Duckworth.

———. 1980. *The Victorians and Ancient Greece*. Cambridge: Harvard University Press.

Johnson, W. R. 1982. *The Idea of Lyric: Lyric Modes in Ancient and Modern Poetry*. Berkeley: University of California Press.

Kelly, Louis. 1979. *The True Interpreter: A History of Translation Practice and Theory in the West.* Oxford: Blackwell.

Kenner, Hugh. 1951. *The Poetry of Ezra Pound.* London: Faber and Faber.

———. 1975. "The Poetics of Error." *MLN* 90:738–46.

———. 1971. *The Pound Era.* Berkeley: University of California Press.

———. 1963. Introduction to *Ezra Pound: Translations.* New York: New Directions.

Kermode, Frank. 1975. *The Classic: Literary Images of Permanence and Change.* New York: Viking.

Kirkwood, G. M. 1974. *Early Greek Monody: The History of a Poetic Type.* Ithaca: Cornell University Press.

Knox, Ronald. 1949. *Trials of a Translator.* New York: Sheed and Ward.

———. 1957. *On English Translation.* Romanes Lectures, Oxford: Clarendon Press.

Kroll, Wilhelm. [1923] 1959, 1968. *Catull.* Stuttgart: Teubner.

Laband, Valery. 1946. *Sous l'invocation de Saint Jerome.* Paris: Gallimard.

Lathrop, Henry B. 1934. *Translations from the Classics from Caxton to Chapman, 1477–1620.* University of Wisconsin Studies in Language and Literature, 34, Madison: University of Wisconsin Press.

Laughlin, James. 1938. "Ezra Pound's Propertius." *Sewanee Review* 46(October–December): 480–91.

Lawendowski, B. P. 1978. "On Semiotic Aspects of Translation." In *Sight, Sound and Sense,* edited by T. Sebeok. 264–82. Bloomington: Indiana University Press.

Lee, M. Owen. 1969. *Word, Sound, and Image in the Odes of Horace.* Ann Arbor: University of Michigan Press.

Lefèvre, André. 1975. *Translating Poetry: Seven Strategies and a Blueprint.* Assen/Amsterdam: Jan Gorcum.

Leishman, J. B. 1956. *Translating Horace.* Oxford: Bruno Cassirer.

Lesky, Albin. 1966. *A History of Greek Literature.* Translated by James Willis and Cornelis de Heer. London: Methuen.

Levin, Harry. 1962. *Refractions.* London and Oxford: Oxford University Press.

Levý, Jiří. 1969. *Die literarische Uebersetzun: Theorie einer Kunstgattung.* Frankfurt: Athenaum.

Lind, L. R. 1957. *Latin Poetry in Verse Translation.* Boston: Houghton Mifflin.

———. 1983. "On 'Modern' Translation." *Classical and Modern Literature* 3(Winter): 69–74.

Lloyd-Jones, Hugh. 1982. *Blood for The Ghosts: Classical Influences in the Nineteenth and Twentieth Centuries.* London: Duckworth.

Luck, G. 1969. *The Latin Love Elegy.* London: Methuen.

Lucot, R. 1961. "Problèmes de creation chez Properce." *Pallas* 10:59–68.

Ludskanov, A. 1975. "A Semiotic Approach to the Theory of Translation." *Language Sciences* 35(April): 5–58.

MacAdam, Alfred. 1975. "Translation as Metaphor." *MLN* 90:747–54.

MacFarlaine, J. W. 1953. "Modes of Translation." *Durham University Journal* 45:77–93.

Mackenna, Stephen. 1936. *The Journal and Letters of Stephen MacKenna.* Edited with a memoir by E. R. Dodds. London: Constable and Co.

Macksey, Richard. 1975. "Introduction: The Deserted Museum." *MLN* 90:731–37.

Macleod, Colin. 1983. *Collected Essays.* Edited by Oliver Taplin. Oxford: Clarendon Press.

Martial. [1903] 1929. *M. Val. Martialis Epigrammata.* Edited by W. M. Lindsay. Oxford: Clarendon Press.

Mason, H. A. 1972. *To Homer Through Pope.* New York: Barnes and Noble.

Matthiesson, F. O. [193] 1965. *Translation, An Elizabethan Art.* Cambridge: Harvard University Press; reprint, New York: Octagon Books.

Messing, A. M. 1975. "Pound's Properties: The Homage and the Damage," in *Poetry and Poetics from Ancient Greece to the Renaissance: Studies in Honor of James Hutton,* edited by G. M. Kilkwood. Ithaca: Cornell University Press.

Michie, James, trans. 1963. *The Odes of Horace.* London: Orion Press.

Miller, Vincent E. 1975. "The Serious Wit of Pound's Homage to Sextus Propertius." *Contemporary Literature* 16(Autumn): 452–62.

Monk, Donald. 1976. "How to Misread: Pound's Use of Translation." in *Ezra Pound: The London Years: 1908–1920,* edited by Philip Grover, 61–88. New York: AMS.

Mounin, Georges. 1963. *Les Problèmes théoretiques de la traduction.* Paris: Gallimard.

———. 1955. *Les Belles infidèles.* Paris: Cahiers de Sud.

Myami, P. 1956. "General Concepts or Laws in Translation." *Modern Language Journal* 40:13–21.

Nabokov, Vladimir. 1941. "The Art of Translation." *The New Republic* 105:160.

———. 1955. "The Problems of Translation: Onegin in English." *Partisan Review* 22:496–512.

Newman, F. W. 1861. *Homeric Translation Theory and Practice.* London: Williams and Norgate.

Newman, J. K. 1967. *Augustus and the New Poetry.* Brussels: Latomus.

Newmark, Peter. 1981. *Approaches to Translation.* London: Pergamon Press.

———. 1973. "Twenty-three Restricted Rules of Translation." *The Incorporated Linguist* 12:9–15.

Nida, Eugene and Charles Tabor. 1969. *The Theory and Practice of Translation.* Leiden: E. J. Brill.

Nisbett, R. G. M. and Margaret Hubbard. 1970. *A Commentary on Horace: Odes (Books I and II).* Oxford: Clarendon Press.

Nixon, Paul. 1927. *Martial and the Modern Epigram. Our Debt to Greece and Rome.* New York: Cooper Square.

Ogilvie, R. M. 1964. *Latin and Greek: A History of the Influence of the Classics on English Life from 1600–1918.* London: Routledge and Kegan Paul.

Page, Denys. 1955. *Sappho and Alcaeus.* Oxford: Clarendon Press.

———. 1958. "Deduke men ha selana." *Journal of Hellenic Studies* 78:84–86.

Palmer, Henrietta R. 1911. *A List of English Editions and Translations of the Classics Printed before 1641.* London Bibliographical Society.

Parks, George G. and Ruth Z. Temple. 1968. *The Literatures of the World in English Translation.* Vol. 1, *The Greek and Latin Literatures.* New York: Frederick Ungar.

Peacock, Alan J. 1980. "Pound, Horace and Canto IV." *English Language Notes* 17(June): 288–92.

Perloff, Marjorie. 1985. *The Dance of the Intellect*. Cambridge: Cambridge University Press.

Pfeiffer, Rudolf. 1976. *History of Classical Scholarship 1300–1850*. Oxford: Clarendon Press.

Popovič, Anton. 1976. *A Dictionary for the Analysis of Literary Translation*. Alberta: University of Alberta, Department of Comparative Literature.

Porter, Peter. 1972. *After Martial*. Oxford: Oxford University Press.

———. 1983. *Collected Poems*. Oxford: Oxford University Press.

Postgate, John P. 1922. *Translation and Translations: Theory and Practice*. London: Bell.

Pound, Ezra. 1929. "Guido's Relations." *The Dial* 86:[559]–68.

———. 1973. "I Gather the Limbs of Osiris." In *Selected Prose 1909–1965*, edited by William Cookson, 19–43. London: Faber and Faber. This article is cited parenthetically in the text as "Osiris."

———. 1951. *The Letters of Ezra Pound. 1907–1941*. Edited by D. D. Paige. London: Faber and Faber. This edition is cited parenthetically in the text as *Letters*.

———. 1935. "Notes on Elizabethan Classicists." In *Make It New*, 95–121. New Haven: Yale University Press. This essay is cited parenthetically in the text as "Notes."

———. 1935. "Translators of Greek" In *Make It New*, 125–56. This essay is cited parenthetically in the text as "Translators."

———. [1953] 1970. *The Translations of Ezra Pound*. London: Faber and Faber; reprinted and enlarged with an introduction by Hugh Kenner. This edition is cited parenthetically in the text as *Translations*.

———. 1930. "Horace." *The Criterion* 9(January): 217–27. This article is cited parenthetically in the text as "Horace."

Propertius. 1977. *Propertius: Elegies I–IV*. Edited by L. Richardson, Jr. Norman: University of Oklahoma Press.

Propertius. 1960. *Sexti Properti Carmina*. Edited by E. A. Barber. Oxford: Clarendon Press.

Quine, W. V. O. 1960. *Word and Object*. Cambridge: MIT Press.

Quinn, K. 1959. *The Catullan Revolution*. Cambridge: Cambridge University Press.

Raffel, Burton, trans. 1983. *The Essential Horace*. With a forward and afterword by W. R. Johnson. San Francisco: North Point Press.

———. 1971. *The Forked Tongue: A Study of the Translation Process*. The Hague: Mouton.

———. 1969. "No Tidbit Love You Outdoors Far as a Bier: Zukofsky's Catullus." *Arion* 8(Autumn): 435–45.

Rescher, N. 1956. "Translation and Philosophic Analysis." *Journal of Philosophy* 53:219–24.

Review of *Homage* in *The New Age*. 26(1919): 82–83.

Rexroth, Kenneth. 1962. *The Greek Anthology*. Ann Arbor: University of Michigan Press.

Richards, I. A. 1932. *Mencius on the Mind: Experiments in Multiple Definition*. London: Routledge and Kegan Paul.

Richardson, Lawrence. 1947. "Ezra Pound's *Homage to Sextus Propertius.*" *Yale Poetry Review* 6 : 21–29.

Rose, Marilyn Gaddis, ed. 1981. *Translation Spectrum: Essays in Theory and Practice.* Binghamton: SUNY Press.

Ross, D. O. 1975. *Backgrounds to Augustan Poetry: Gallus, Elegy, and Rome.* Cambridge: Cambridge University Press.

————. 1970. *Style and Tradition in Catullus.* Cambridge: Harvard University Press.

Rudd, Niall. 1976. *Lines of Inquiry: Studies in Latin Poetry.* London: Cambridge University Press.

Ruthven, K. K. 1969. *A Guide to Ezra Pound's Personae (1926).* Berkeley: University of California Press.

Rydbeck, Lars. 1969. "Sappho's *Phainetai moi kenos.*" *Hermes* 97 : 161–66.

Sandys, Sir J. E. [1908] 1964. *A History of Classical Scholarship.* Cambridge: Cambridge University Press.

Sapir, Edward. 1956. *Culture, Language, and Personality.* Berkeley: University of California Press.

Savory, Theodore Horace. [1957] 1968. *The Art of Translation.* London: Cape.

Scamuzzi, U. 1966. "Contributo ad una obietiva conoscenza della vita e dell' opera di Marco Valerio Marziale." *Revista di Studi Classici* 14 : 149–207.

Schneeman, Peter. 1972. *Ezra Pound and the Act of Translation.* Ph.D. diss., University of Minnesota.

Selver, Paul. 1966. *The Art of Translating Poetry.* London: Baker.

Shackleton Bailey, D. R. 1956. *Propertiana.* Cambridge: Cambridge University Press.

Shaefer, E. 1966. *Das Verhältnis von Erlebnis und Kunstgestalt bei Catull, Hermes Einzelschriften.* Heft 18. Wiesbaden: Steiner.

Shaffer, E. S., 1984. "Editor's Introduction." *Comparative Criticism* 6 : xii–xxvii.

Sisson, C. H. 174. *In the Trojan Ditch.* Cheadle: Carcanet Press.

Smith, K. F. 1920. *Martial the Epigrammatist and Other Essays.* Baltimore: Johns Hopkins University Press.

Solmsen, F. 1948. "Propertius and Horace." *Classical Philology* 43 : 105–9.

Speirs, John. 1935. "Mr. Pound's Propertius," *Scrutiny* 3(March): 409–18.

Steiner, George. 1975. *After Babel: Aspects of Language and Translation.* London: Oxford University Press.

————, ed. 1966. *Poem into Poem* (formerly, *The Penguin Book of Modern Verse Translation*). Harmondsworth: Penguin.

Steiner, T. R. 1975. *English Translation Theory, 1950–1800.* Amsterdam and Assen: Van Gorcum.

Stoneman, Richard. 1982. *Daphne into Laurel: Translations of Classical Poetry from Chaucer to the Present.* London: Duckworth.

Storrs, Ronald. 1959. *Ad Pyrrham: A Polyglot Collection of Translations of Horace Odes 1.5.* Oxford: Oxford University Press.

Sullivan, John P. 1969. "Ezra Pound and the Classics." In *New Approaches to Ezra Pound,* edited by Eva Hesse, 215–41. London: Faber and Faber.

————. 1964. *Ezra Pound and Sextus Propertius: A Study in Creative Translation.* London: Faber and Faber.

———. 1976. *Propertius: A Critical Introduction.* Cambridge: Cambridge University Press.

Terrell, Carroll, ed. 1980. *Basil Bunting: Man and Poet.* Orono, Maine: National Poetry Foundation.

Thomas, Ronald E. 1981. "The Catullan Landscape in Pound's Poetry." *Contemporary Poetry* 4(Spring): 66–78.

———. 1983. *The Latin Masks of Ezra Pound.* Ann Arbor: UMI Research Press.

Tomlinson, Charles, ed. 1980. *The Oxford Book of Verse in English Translation.* Oxford: Oxford University Press.

———. 1983, *Poetry and Metamorphosis.* Cambridge: Cambridge University Press.

Toury, Gideon. 1980. *In Search of a Theory of Translation.* Tel Aviv: Porter Institute for Poetics and Semiotics.

Trankle, H. 1960. *Die Sprachkunst des Properz und die Trandition der lateinischen Dictersprache, Hermes Einzelschriften.* Heft 15. Wiesbaden: Steiner.

Turner, Mark. 1976. "Propertius Through the Looking Glass: A Fragmentary Glance at the Construction of Pound's *Homage.*" *Paideuma* 5:241–65.

Tytler, Alexander [Lord Woodhouslee]. 1791. *Essays on the Principles of Translation.* London.

West, David. 1967. *Reading Horace.* Edinburgh: Edinburgh University Press.

Whipple, T. K. 1925, reprint 1970. *Martial and the English Epigram from Sir Thomas Wyatt to Ben Jonson.* New York: Phaeton Press.

Wilamowitz–Moellendorff, U. von. 1982. *History of Classical Scholarship.* Translated by Alan Harris and edited by Hugh Lloyd-Jones. London: Duckworth.

Wilkinson, L. P. 1970. *Golden Latin Artistry.* Cambridge: Cambridge University Press.

———. 1945. *Horace and His Lyric Poetry.* Cambridge: Cambridge University Press.

Will, Frederick. 1975. "Dead Stones in Our Mouths: A Review of Two New Books on Translation." *MLN* 90:972–82.

———. 1973. *The Knife in the Stone.* The Hague: Mouton.

Williams, Gordon. 1968. *Tradition and Originality in Roman Poetry.* Oxford: Clarendon Press.

Wills, Garry. 1967. "Sappho 31 and Catullus 51." *Greek, Roman and Byzantine Studies* 8:167–97.

Wimmel, W. 1960. *Kallimachos in Rom: Die Nachfolge seines apologetischen Dichtens in der Augusteerzeit, Hermes Einzelschriften.* Heft 16. Wiesbaden: Steiner.

Wiseman, T. P. 1969. *Catullan Questions.* Leicester: Leicester University Press.

Woodman, A. J. 1966. "Some Implications of Otium in Cat. 51, 13–16." *Latomus* 25:217–66.

Zukofsky, Louis and Celia, trans. 1969. *Catullus.* London: Cape Goliard Press.

Index